MEMORY GIFTS

MEMORY GIFTS

Preserving Your Treasured Past
in Special Ways

Marie Browning

Sterling Publishing Co., Inc.
New York

PROLIFIC IMPRESSIONS PRODUCTION STAFF:

Editor: Mickey Baskett
Copy: Phyllis Mueller
Graphics: Dianne Miller, Karen Turpin
Styling: Laney Crisp McClure
Photography: Jerry Mucklow
Administration: Jim Baskett

Library of Congress Cataloging-in-Publication Data

Browning, Marie.
    Memory gifts: Preserving your treasured past in special ways/Marie Browning.
        p. cm.
    Includes index.
    ISBN 0-8069-3933-8
    1. Handicraft. 2. Photographs – Conservation and restoration. 3. Souvenirs (Keepsakes) 4. Gifts. I. Title.
TT857.B76 2000
745.5 – dc21   99-054257
                                                        CIP

Published by Sterling Publishing Company, Inc.
387 Park Avenue South, New York, N.Y. 10016
Produced by Prolific Impressions, Inc.
160 South Candler St., Decatur, GA 30030
© 1999 by Prolific Impressions, Inc.
Distributed in Canada by Sterling Publishing
c/o Canadian Manda Group, One Atlantic Avenue, Suite 105
Toronto, Ontario, Canada M6K 3E7
Distributed in Great Britain and Europe by Cassell PLC
Wellington House, 125 Strand, London WC2R 0BB, England
Distributed in Australia by Capricorn Link (Australia) Pty. Ltd.
P.O. Box 6651, Baulkham Hills, Business Centre,
NSW 2153 Australia

Printed in China
All rights reserved
Sterling ISBN 0-8069-3933-8

ACKNOWLEDGEMENTS

Marie Browning thanks the following manufacturers, stores, and individuals for their generous contributions of materials used in this book:

Plaid Enterprises
Norcross, GA 30091-7600
www.plaidonline.com
For acrylic paints, acrylic glazes, stencil gels, stencils, acrylic varnishes, and Picture This photo transfer medium:

Delta Technical Coatings, Inc.
Whittier, CA 90601-1505
www.deltacrafts.com
For acrylic paints, SoftTint colors for the Tint O' Pauge technique, stencil paints, stencils, acrylic varnishes:

Environmental Technology, Inc.
Fields Landing, CA 95537
www.eti-usa.com
For the two-part pour-on resin coating, Envirotec:

Walnut Hollow
Dodgeville, WI 53533-2112
For wooden document and keepsake boxes, wooden frames, desk top triptych, wooden plaques, wooden discs, wooden memory albums:

Polyform
Elk Grove Village, IL 60007
For Premo! Sculpey polymer clay:

Fiskars
Wausau, WI 54402-8027
www.fiskars.com
For decorative scissors, slide trimmer, art knives, cutting mats, circle cutters:

Boutique Trims
South Lyon, MI 48178
For metal charms and jewelry findings:

Kunin Felt
Hampton, NH
Embossed and brushed felt.

SpotPen
Las Cruces, NM 88005
For dye pens for hand-tinting photographs:

Personal Stamp Exchange
www.psxstamps.com
Art rubber stamps and accessories, package and box templates

Magenta
Mont-Saint-Hilaire, Quebec, Canada
Art rubber stamps and accessories, calendar stamps, calendar blanks

Folk Art Connection
www.folkartconnection.com
Brentwood Bay, BC, Canada
For wooden coaster tray, wooden calendar, wooden coasters, wooden blocks, and tile and wood trivet:

A Bride's Marketplace
Calgary, Alberta, Canada
For microwave flower presses, beveled glass, mica sheets, and copper tape:

House Dressing Co.
Sidney, BC, Canada
For image transfer markers:

ABOUT THE AUTHOR

Marie Browning

Marie Browning is a consummate craft designer, making a career of designing products, writing books and articles, plus teaching and demonstrating. You may have already been charmed by her creative designs and not even been aware; as she has designed stencils, stamps, transfers, and a variety of other products for national art & craft supply companies.

You may also have enjoyed books and articles by Marie. She is the author of three other books published by Sterling, *Natural Soapmaking* (1998), *Handcrafted Journals, Albums, Scrapbooks, & More* (1999), and *Making Glorious Gifts From the Garden* (1999). Her articles and designs have appeared in *Handcraft Illustrated*, *Better Homes & Gardens*, *Canadian Stamper*, *Great American Crafts*, *All American Crafts*, and in numerous project books published by Plaid Enterprises, Inc.

Browning earned a Fine Arts Diploma from Camosun College and attended the University of Victoria. She is a Certified Professional Demonstrator, a professional affiliate of the Canadian Craft and Hobby Association, and a member of the Stencil Artisan's League and the Society of Craft Designers.

Marie Browning lives, gardens, and crafts on Vancouver Island in Canada. She and her husband Scott have three children: Katelyn, Lena, and Jonathan. ∞

CONTENTS

INTRODUCTION
page 8

COLLECTING, ORGANIZING & PRESERVING MEMORABILIA
page 10

TECHNIQUES FOR PRESERVING YOUR MEMORIES
page 12 - 31

Cutting & Cropping
page 12

Photocopying
page 14

Color Tinting Photographs
page 16

Transferring Photographs to Fabric
page 17

Transferring Photographs to Polymer Clay
page 18

Using Photographs on Candles
page 20

Decoupage Techniques
page 21

Using Resin to Preserve Memories
page 22

Paper Image Transferring
page 24

Preserving Memories Under Glass
page 26

Preserving Memories Under Mica
page 27

Decorative Paint Techniques
page 28

Natural Accents - Preserving Flowers
page 30

PRESERVING MEMORIES PROJECTS
pages 32 -125

Boxes & Albums for Photos & Memories
page 34

Using Memories in Home Deccor
page 40

Trays & Coasters
page 57

Framing & Displaying Photos
page 64

Calendars
page 82

Fabric Memories
page 86

Jewelry & Wearable Memories
page 92

Gifts & Wraps
page 102

Ornaments
page 112

Use Treasured Photographs to Make Gifts for Family and Friends, Home Decorative Objects, and Wearables.

Memory crafting – creating elegant heirlooms with treasures from the past and present – is popular because the projects you make can be meaningful remembrances and keepsakes. This book includes wonderful ideas for preserving and displaying photographs and memorabilia and provides instructions for a variety of memory crafting techniques, including putting photographs on glazed ceramics, wooden plaques, fabrics, paper, canvas, and under glass.

Memory projects have value because they preserve special times in your family's history.

As our lives get more hurried and high-tech, the act of touching the past and the effort and time put into memory projects have value because they preserve special times in your family's history. Everyone, I'm sure, has a drawer full of family photographs. This book will give you the incentive you need to pull those photos from the drawer and create lasting keepsakes.

I am thankful that my ancestors felt it important to preserve their life stories in photographs. They inspired me to create family treasures and traditions that my children can share with their families. Now I share them with you.

Marie Browning

COLLECTING, ORGANIZING, AND PRESERVING MEMORABILIA

Getting all your photographs, memorabilia, and treasures organized so that you can create heirlooms is something we are constantly telling ourselves we need to do. This book will help you get a good start on this overwhelming task.

Keeping your photographs in an organized system is preserving the past and writing your family's history for future generations. With the popularity of memory book crafting, many of us have already started to collect and organize our treasures. Found treasures such as shells from a beach holiday, a ticket stub from a evening at the theater, pressed flowers from your graduation, or a ribbon from a school sporting event are valuable keepsakes that deserve a special place.

I found the easiest way to systematize my treasures was to use large photo boxes and file cards to sort and document my photographs and other memorabilia. In storage boxes, you can keep volumes of photographs, papers, and other memorabilia that you and your family can revisit over and over, and even more important, you'll keep it all together and out of harm's way. Since I use photocopies, not actual photographs, for crafts projects, I wanted to make sure the picture I want to use is easy to find and easy to replace.

Keeping your photographs in an organized system is preserving the past and writing your family's history for future generations.

Make sure you clearly date and label each photograph with names, places, and occasions when preparing your files. I find writing the details on an acid-free label and placing the label on the back of the photograph is the best way to identify the photographs without damaging the image. When you create with these photographs, you'll want this information for labeling and documenting your projects.

Preserving the Past

Today people are more conscious of using "acid free" materials to help preserve photographs for future generations. (The correct terminology is "pH balanced" – all materials have a little trace of acid, and it is the balance that makes them safe.) By all means, use "acid free" materials available whenever possible for your memory crafting, but be more concerned about preserving your original photographs.

Color photographs of President Kennedy from the 1960s, carefully stored in sterile, museum quality environments are fading away, not because of the storage materials, but because the color photographs themselves are unstable. Black and white prints made during the Civil War, however, are holding up beautifully. The quality of color prints has improved greatly over the last 30 years, but it is still wise to put a roll of black and white film into your camera each year and snap photos of your family to ensure that some of your photographs will stand the test of time.

Documenting and Labeling with Journaling

Documenting and labeling your memory craft projects with names, dates, and sayings – called "journaling" – can provide meaning and significance as well as additional decorative elements. Gold and silver paint pens, permanent felt tip markers, stenciled letters, and rubber stamp alphabets all can be used to add personal touches. I find books of phrases, quotations, and expressions helpful and inspirational when fashioning my projects. The books often include artistic alphabet styles as well.

Techniques for Preserving Your Memories
Cutting and Cropping Photographs

You'll need to cut and crop your photocopied prints before creating your projects. Having the right tools for the job helps make this experience more successful. A slide trimmer is the easiest and fastest way to crop pictures. Cutting your images into circles, stars, or other creative shapes can add a special touch to your projects. Another way to trim your images to fit flush to a surface is by sanding the edges with sandpaper. Sanding cuts the paper and gives a neat, professional-looking edge. You can also cut out backgrounds and other areas of prints using small sharp craft or decoupage scissors.

Cropping Tips
- Remove background that does not improve or add anything to the image.
- Highlight the focal point of the photograph without crowding it.
- Don't cut off people's feet or cut too close to the tops of their heads.
- Choose images for decoupage that have simple, large shapes and clear, easy to cut outlines. It is much easier to cut images from a photocopy than from an actual photograph. Cut very carefully, using sharp crafting scissors.

Cutting Tools

Perfect cutting and cropping are the first steps to perfect projects. Good sharp knives and paper trimmers are best for trimming and cropping – scissors won't provide straight, sharp edges. Make sure you have a supply of blades for your cutting tools to ensure you'll always have a sharp cutting edge.

- An **ART KNIFE** or **CRAFT KNIFE** with a replaceable pointed blade is essential. It is an all-purpose cutting knife for trimming photographs and cutting card stock.
- **PAPER CUTTERS** such as a **guillotine paper cutter** or a **paper trimmer with a sliding blade** make it easy to precisely trim photographs. You also can use your art knife for this purpose, but a paper trimmer makes the job much easier and faster. Slide trimmers and paper cutters are readily available at reasonable prices.
- **SHARP SMALL CRAFT SCISSORS** are needed for decorative treatments such as decoupage.
- **PAPER SCISSORS** are always a must for trimming papers, snipping ribbons, and cords, and other crafting chores.
- **DECORATIVE EDGE SCISSORS** are fun to use and available in a variety of styles.
- **SELF-HEALING CUTTING MAT** with a printed grid protects your work surface and provides very accurate cuts. The mat surface seals itself after each cut, so your knife won't follow a previous cut. The mats with 1", 1/2", and 1/4" grid markings make measuring and cutting perfectly square corners a breeze. The cutting mats range in size from 9" x 12" to ones that cover an entire table top. Buy the biggest mat your budget will allow.
- **STRAIGHT-EDGE METAL RULER** with a cork backing is needed for making perfectly straight cuts. Wooden and plastic rulers can slide, and your knife will cut into them. A ruler 12" to 18" is suitable.

- **ROTARY CUTTERS** are great to use when cutting fabric. They can cut through several layers of fabric with ease, creating perfect straight edges.
- The **CIRCLE CUTTER** is an inexpensive tool that cuts perfect circles in a variety of sizes. Use the cutter with a self-healing cutting mat.
- **SANDPAPER** can be used to create a flush fit when applying a photograph to a wooden plaque, tray, coaster or other surface. Cut the image at least 1/2" larger on all sides than your surface. Using white glue or decoupage medium, adhere the image to the surface. Let dry completely. Hold the sandpaper at a 45 degree angle to the surface and sand the paper until it is cut through, being sure not to scratch your image. This method gives a precise, professional-looking edge and takes away the guess work in cutting an image the exact size of the surface.

*Pictured at right: (1)Straight-edge metal ruler, (2)Rotary cutter, (3)Decorative edge scissors, 4)All purpose paper scissors, (5)Paper trimmer with sliding blade, (6)Craft knife (**putting the blade in a cork when not in use is a great safety tip and it will also keep the blade from getting knicked or the point from being broken.**)*

Photocopying

Most of the projects in the book are created from copied images. Using copies gives you flexibility – you can change the size and color easily; you can create multiple images of the same photo to use. If you make a mistake, the original is safe. Besides using photocopied images, I also used a scanner and a computer printer to reproduce some images. With a computer, you can scan images on photographic paper or textured canvas paper.

Tips for Photocopying

I recommend you get to know the people at a photocopy shop and learn what their machine can do. If they recognize you as a regular customer, you'll find them more willing to accommodate an unusual request and more obliging in experimenting with their $15,000 machine. While creating the projects for this book, I had the employees at my local photocopy shop try out a variety of papers and techniques. They also let me take the manual home so I could study it. I learned what's possible and what the machines can and cannot do. Most of my "experiments" worked beautifully and did no damage to the machine, and in the process of helping me, the operators became more knowledgeable about their equipment.

Gang-up Sheets:

Color photocopies can be expensive, so ganging up (copying more than one at a time) your photographs can save you money. Place as many photographs as you can fit on a letter or legal size piece of paper, using double sided tape to hold them in place, and photocopy them as one. Remove the tape immediately after the copies are made. Ganging up black and white photographs together and color photographs together, rather than mixing them, will make better copies.

Shown here are two techniques. (Techniques 1:) Both the examples use gang-up sheets. Photocopying more than one photo on a sheet will save time and money. (Technique 2:) The same original photos were used to create both the black and white copies as well as the color copies.

Color photocopies look like the real thing. Here original color photographs were also used to create monotone prints such as the sepia, red, blue and purple shown.

Copying Black and White Photographs:

You'll have more interesting images if you copy black and white photographs on a color photocopier – you will get a clearer copy showing gray tone shadows and white highlights. A black and white copier reproduces only black and white tones, resulting in an inferior image. A color photocopier will pick up the beautiful sepia tones of old black and white photographs, too.

Enlarging and Reducing:

All color photocopiers are able to enlarge and reduce your images. You will want to reduce photographs for jewelry pieces and enlarge them for trays and wearable pieces. When you are ready to photocopy the images, carefully measure your project and tell the copier operator the exact size you want. Measuring carefully means you'll need only to make one copy.

Reverse Imaging:

You will want to have a reverse image on transfer paper

Here photos were copied onto a variety of papers, including vellum that makes a translucent print.

made of photographs that you want to iron on fabric or transfer to polymer clay. (It's especially important to reverse the image if there are letters or numbers in the photo.) Reverse image copying also is necessary for images you're planning to transfer to paper.

Monotone Images:

Many color photocopiers can copy your image in single color tones. I used this technique to change color photographs into warm sepia-toned images that look similar to old photographs. You can also change color photographs into black and white images and enhance them with color tinting techniques.

Repeat Images

Many color photocopiers can make multiple prints on a single sheet of paper. This is useful for photo card making, practicing color tinting, and creating three-dimensional photos. Ask the operator if this is possible.

SPECIALTY PAPERS

Several types of papers are available for use in color photocopiers. Ask the photocopy operator which specialty papers are compatible with their particular machine.

- **Transfer paper** is used to carry your images to fabric with a household iron or to carry images to polymer clay. Transfer paper is available at color photocopy centers and from craft and fabric stores.
- **Clear transparencies** are generally used for businesses and schools to project images with overhead projectors. Photographs printed on transparencies make wonderful images for window pictures and night light and candle lanterns.
- **Parchment** and **vellum** papers can go through the copier with attractive results. Vellum is available in colors as well as imbedded with sparkles and glitter for a beautiful festive image.
- **High gloss paper** that simulates actual photographic paper can be used when you wish a more realistic photo reproduction.

SCANNING AND PRINTING WITH A COMPUTER

All these techniques, and a lot more can be done with a home computer, a flat bed scanner and a good quality color printer. Read the manuals that come with the machines and explore the numerous software programs available.

Color Tinting Photographs

Hand coloring can bring brilliance to an old photograph and soften the look of new prints. In this book, I used two techniques that are easy, require no experience, and produce great results the first time. SpotPens are used on original black and white photographs. Tint O' Pauge is for coloring photocopied images. Other photo tinting techniques include professional photo oils, colored pencils, paint markers, and oil based pastel crayons.

SpotPens

SpotPens are fun and easy to use. The pens work on both glossy and matte surfaces and the coloring system actually penetrates the emulsion of the photograph and becomes part of the print. SpotPens color requires no protective coating and dries on the print in about half an hour. A starter kit with pens, a remover pen for mistakes, a pre-moistening solution, and a practice print is available at many shops where photo supplies are sold. I prefer to keep colors soft, but more intense coloring also can be produced. Follow the simple instructions to give your black and white photographs a softly colored, nostalgic look. The colors are transparent and shadows are created when you color over the print. Use lighter pens on white areas and darker colors on the deep shadows and black areas.

Here's How

Preparation:
1. Select a photograph to tint. Choose one with large elements and good contrast of light and dark areas.
2. Before you use the coloring pens, you must soften the tips so they do not scratch the print and so the colors go on evenly. Soften the tip by rubbing it vigorously on a piece of card stock for about 60 seconds.
3. Dilute 1 teaspoon of the pre-moistening solution with 32 oz. water. Apply the solution to the surface of the print with a sponge.

Application:
1. Starting with the largest element in your photograph, apply the color in light circular strokes, gradually building up the color. The colors in the pens are lightly tinted, so it may take several applications to build up the desired intensity.
2. When you are satisfied with the coloring, sponge over the whole print with a light coat of pre-moistening solution. Let air dry 30 minutes.
3. Photocopy the colored print for your memory projects.

Tips
- If you make a mistake, use the dye removal pen to immediately correct it. Once the dye has set, it is permanent and impossible to remove.
- When coloring faces, avoid the teeth and the whites of the eyes.
- To keep the photograph moist as you work, re-apply the pre-moistening solution as needed.

Tint O' Pauge

This easy way to achieve the nostalgic look of tinted photos was developed by Nancy Tribolet and is available at many art and craft stores. Tint O' Pauge uses a soft, transparent paint medium to color photocopied prints. The method is easy to do and quite inexpensive. Mistakes are easily corrected. Prints are colored after they have been adhered to the surface. If you are unable to find SoftTint colors, you can use diluted acrylic glaze colors for similar results.

Here's How

Preparation:
1. Choose your photograph and copy it on a color copier, using the black and white setting for colored prints.
2. Adhere the print to your surface using a decoupage medium. Let dry.
3. Apply an even coat of a matte acrylic varnish to seal the print. Let dry.

Application:
1. Dilute the SoftTint colors with water and wash them over the print. The result should be a light transparent wash that the shadows and highlights can be seen through. Let dry completely.
2. Apply a coat of acrylic varnish to seal.

Tips:
- If you cannot see the photo details, you are applying too much paint.
- If you make a mistake, use a damp cotton swab to gently rub the color away.

Transferring Photographs to Fabric

I have included two techniques, using transfer paper and transfer medium, to transfer photographs to fabric. Both are effortless and relatively inexpensive.

USING IRON AND PEEL TRANSFER PAPER

High resolution transfer papers are available for both computer printers and color copiers. The paper for color copiers can only be used in a color copier, not a black and white copier. Many copy shops sell transfer paper to use with their machines. You also can purchase packages of transfer paper from craft stores and fabric shops. The package comes with instructions for the copy shop and includes a toll free number for questions or problems. Be sure to ask the photocopy machine operator to reverse the image before copying.

Instructions for transferring the image using a home iron also are included in the package. Your ironing surface should be hard and smooth; most ironing boards are fine. Lower the board so you can apply pressure to the transfer while ironing.

Here's How

1. Trim the print on the transfer paper 1/4" around the entire image.
2. Pre-heat the iron on the highest setting suitable for the fabric with no steam. Iron the fabric to heat it.
3. Place the image face down on the fabric and iron over the transfer paper, applying firm pressure over the entire transfer area. Iron for about 30 seconds, keeping the iron moving at all times to prevent scorching.
4. Peel away the transfer paper immediately while it is still very hot.

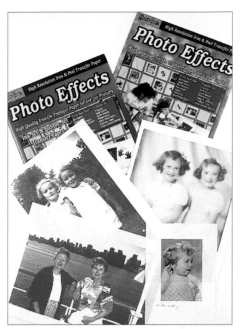

Iron and peel transfer paper

USING TRANSFER MEDIUM

Transfer medium is a clear, water-based acrylic medium that permanently adheres a photocopied image to fabrics. You must use a color copy, not an original photograph. Be sure to ask the photocopier operator to make a reverse image copy. Prints transferred using transfer medium can be washed.

Here's How

Preparation:
1. Wash and dry the fabric.
2. Protect your work surface with freezer paper. Cut a piece of freezer paper larger than the size of the transfer and iron the freezer paper to the wrong side of the fabric, with the shiny side of the paper against the fabric. This prevents the medium from soaking through the fabric.

Apply a thick coat of medium to the front of the photocopied image.

Transfer:
1. Trim the photocopied image to size and place face up on the work surface.
2. Brush a very thick coat of the transfer medium on the print – it should be about 1/16" thick, or the thickness of a dime.
3. Place the coated copy on the fabric, right side down. Cover with a paper towel. Using the bottle the transfer medium came in, lightly roll over the entire copy.
4. Remove the paper towel and blot excess medium from the fabric. Let dry 24 to 48 hours.
5. When the transfer medium is completely dry, use a sponge to saturate the copy paper with warm water. Let sit a few minutes. With a slightly damp sponge, firmly rub off the paper. Use a circular scrubbing motion and repeat until all the paper is removed. You may want to let it dry in between scrubbings to help you see where the paper needs to be removed. Let dry 72 hours.

To clean: Wash the fabric in cool water on the gentle cycle. Machine dry on low. Do not iron directly on the transferred image – use a pressing cloth or iron on the reverse side. Do not dry clean.

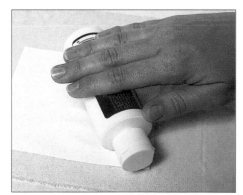

Place the coated image face down on the fabric and roll out any air bubbles.

Transferring Photographs to Polymer Clay

You also can use transfer paper to print images on polymer clay to create ornaments and wearable pins. The technique is simple, but attention to all the steps is important for success. I reversed the images and reduced the photographs quite a bit to make images 1" to 2" high.

You'll Need

- An image printed on transfer paper
- White or light colored polymer clay (White gives the sharpest image, but cream, translucent, and beige also can be used.)
- A hard acrylic brayer
- A spoon
- A sharp blade
- A glazed tile to use as a work surface

If you wish to add a decorative metallic frame to the clay, you will also need:

- A small decorative stamp
- Metallic pigment powders
- A soft brush

Here's How

1. Trim the print to the size and shape you wish to transfer. Using templates, you can cut the image into an oval, a circle, a square, or a star shape. You can also cut out elements from the image and transfer them for interesting results.
2. Preheat your oven to the temperature recommended by the polymer clay manufacturer.
3. Condition the clay well according to package instructions and roll out with the brayer to a thickness of 1/4" to 1/8" and at least 1/2" larger all around than the printed image. Be sure the clay is completely smooth, with no air pockets or indentations.
4. Place the clay on the glazed tile. Place the print, image side down, on the clay. Using the back of a

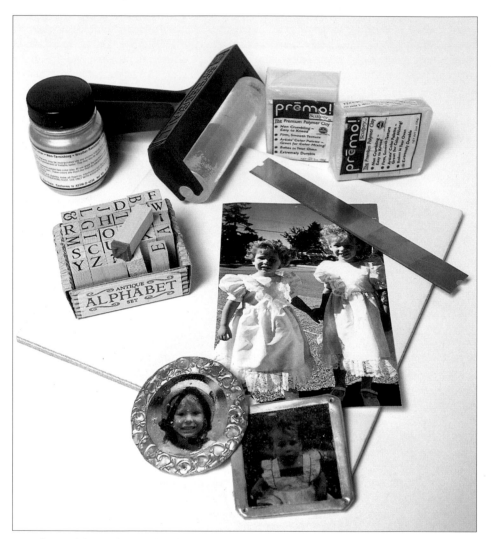

Supplies and finished examples of transferring images to polymer clay.

spoon or a bone burnisher, rub the back of the print to press it into the clay. Go over the print several times to make sure the paper is pressed firmly against the clay. If the image is not pressed into the clay, it will not transfer completely.
5. With the paper print still in place, use a sharp blade to trim the clay 1/4" to 1/2" larger than the paper. If you wish to add holes for hangers, place them now with a toothpick. Do not remove the paper print.
6. To make a "frame," use a small decorative stamp to press a decorative border around the paper print. Use alphabet stamps to impress names or sentiments.

7. Lightly brush powdered pigments on the border, using the soft brush. The pigments will adhere to the clay, giving a soft metallic finish.

8. Place the tile with the clay, paper print still in place, in the preheated oven. Bake 10 minutes.

9. Remove from oven. Slowly remove the paper from the clay. Return the tile and clay to the oven to complete baking according to manufacturer's instructions.

10. Remove from the oven and let cool. If there are spots where the image did not adhere, touch up these areas with permanent felt markers.

Trim the print to the size and shape you wish to transfer.

Roll out clay with the brayer.

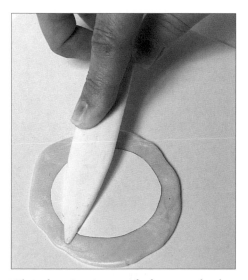

Place the print, image side down, on the clay and burnish it with a bone burnisher or the back of a spoon.

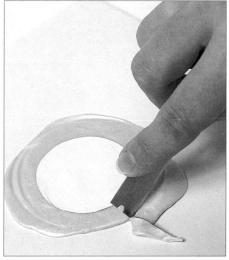

Use a sharp blade to trim the clay.

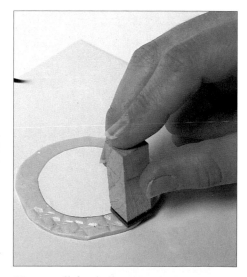

Use a small decorative stamp to press a decorative border around the paper print.

Using Photographs on Candles

Photos and sentiments on a candle make a romantic and elegant gift to celebrate or remember a special event.

You'll Need

- A white or cream short pillar candle (smaller candles are easier for beginners)
- Paraffin wax
- A container deep enough to hold enough wax to completely submerge the candle (I usually use large, clean tins)
- A pot with water that is large enough to hold the wax container

- Wax paper
- A photocopy of the photo you wish to use, trimmed to fit on your candle (You can add sentiments, names, or dates by writing them on white bond paper with permanent markers.)
- A paint brush
- A piece of nylon stocking

Here's How

Preparation:

To find out how much wax you will need to melt and to be sure your container is large enough (you don't want the wax to overflow!), do the following exercise:

1. Place your candle in the tin. Pour in water until the candle is covered. (You will need to hold down the candle as it will want to float to the top.)
2. Take out the candle and mark the water level on the outside of the tin with a permanent marker. Pour out the water and dry the candle and tin.
3. Place the tin inside a pot of water. Melt wax in the tin, adding wax until it reaches the mark. Keep the wax in the water bath so it stays melted.
4. If you wish to add sentiments, names, or dates, write them on bond paper.
5. Cover a work surface large enough to hold the candle with wax paper.

Adhering and Dipping:

1. With a paint brush, paint a little wax on the candle where you wish to place the image. Position the print over the wax.
2. Brush on more wax to completely adhere the photocopy print to the candle. Make sure the print is flush against the surface of the candle. Add sentiments, dates, and names printed on paper, adhering the paper to the candle the same way. Let set.
3. Dip the entire candle in the wax. Use a smooth motion when dipping and do not hesitate during the dip. Repeat once if you like – dipping more than twice will obscure the image.
4. Remove the candle and place on wax paper. Let the wax shell cool and harden over the print. It will look cloudy when it first comes out but will dry clear.
5. Buff the finished candle with a piece of a nylon stocking. ∞

Here a photocopy of a dried flower is adhered to the candle with melted wax.

After print is adhered it is dipped into hot wax to coat it.

Decoupage Techniques

You will need basic decoupage skills for many of the projects in this book. Perfectly trimmed images and careful gluing will result in heirloom quality projects that you will be proud to display and give as gifts.

Here's How

Step One: Cut

Trim away excess paper around the image you wish to decoupage. Use an art knife and cutting board to remove inside areas before cutting around the outer edges. Use small, sharp, pointed scissors and hold the scissors at a 45 degree angle to create a tiny beveled edge on the cut paper. (The beveled edge helps the image adhere snugly against the surface.) Move the print, not the scissors as you cut. It is much easier to cut images from photocopies than from photographs.

Step Two: Glue

Cover your work surface with freezer paper to protect it. Lightly coat the back of the cutout with decoupage medium, using a 1" foam brush. Position the cutout on the surface and smooth it with your fingers, pushing out wrinkles and air bubbles. Allow to dry.

Step Three: Finish

Apply two to three coats of decoupage medium to the surface, using a foam brush. The finish appears cloudy when wet, but will dry crystal clear. If you are

Gather tools and supplies

planning to finish your project with a pour-on resin coating, seal the decoupaged surface with a coat of thin bodied white glue.

Cutting

Gluing

Finishing

Using Resin to Preserve Memories

Using a Two-Part Resin Pour-On Coating gives projects a hard, waterproof, professional-looking finish with a depth and luster equal to 50 coats of varnish and a practical, easy to clean surface. Trays, coasters, plaques, decorative plates, ornaments, and vases all benefit from this durable glossy finish. It's easy to do and the results are spectacular.

You'll Need

- Pour-on resin coating that comes in two parts, a resin and a hardener
- Thin bodied white glue that dries clear
- Photocopied images and other memorabilia
- Rubber cement or masking tape

All these items will be discarded after use:

- A mixing cup
- A wooden stir stick
- An inexpensive foam brush or glue brush
- Freezer paper or wax paper to protect your work surface
- Plastic or paper cups to prop up your project and keep it off the work surface

Tips

- Your work surface should be level, in a warm area, and free of dust.
- The item you wish to coat should be dry and free of dust or grease.
- Mix only as much of the resin coating as you can use at one time; you cannot save what's left over. The resin coating has a self-leveling quality that is attained when you use enough to flood the surface. It is better to mix too much rather than too little. A 4 oz. kit covers up to one square foot.
- The coating will drip off the sides of the project, so protect the underside by brushing on some rubber cement or lining the bottom edges with masking tape.
- If drips occur on an unprotected surface, they can be sanded off when the finish has cured.

Here's How

Preparation:

1. Prepare and protect your work area.

See page 40 for project instructions

2. Adhere photocopies, newspaper clippings, and other memorabilia to the surface with decoupage medium. Let dry.
3. Seal the surface of all decoupaged items with a coat of thin bodied white glue. Let dry. Note: Photographs and images printed on photographic paper do not need to be sealed.
4. Mix the coating. It comes in two parts, the resin and the hardener. Measure exactly one part resin and one part hardener in a disposable container. Mix vigorously with a wooden stick for two minutes until thoroughly blended.

Gather your supplies and tools for project.

continued from page 22

Incomplete mixing can result in a soft finish that won't harden properly. Do not be concerned if bubbles form in the mixture; the bubbles can be removed after the coating is poured.

Application:

1. As soon as the coating is mixed, pour it over the surface of your project. Spread where necessary, using a brush. You will have about 10 minutes to work before it starts to set up.
2. After about five minutes, the air bubbles created by mixing will rise to the surface. The bubbles can be removed (de-gassed) easily and effectively by gently blowing on them until they disappear. (The carbon dioxide in your breath breaks ups the bubbles.) Avoid inhaling fumes as you de-gas the bubbles.
3. Discard the mixing cup, the stir stick, and the brush to clean up. Allow your project to cure for a full 72 hours to a hard and permanent finish.

Mix the two parts of the resin together.

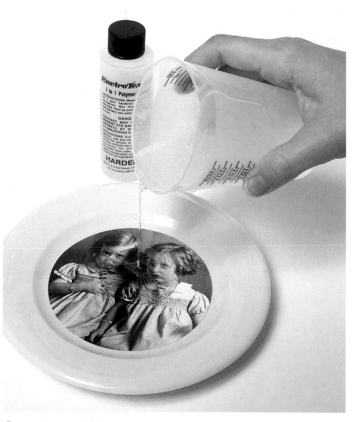

Pour resin over project.

Paper Image Transferring

This transferring technique produces a soft, muted image. The image is "printed" on the paper by releasing the color toner of the photocopy with a lacquer based pen. With this method, it's easy to create aesthetically pleasing cards, labels, and place cards. (I especially like to transfer photocopies of fresh flowers.) After you have mastered transferring colored prints, move on to black and white prints and color them with pencil crayons for another romantic look. WARNING: The fumes can be a little strong. Work in a well-ventilated area.

You'll Need

- Smooth paper (Plain white bond works best, but heavier watercolor papers give a beautiful muted image.)
- Color photocopies, reverse printed
- A release pen (This is a lacquer-based marker sold as a "blender marker" in the graphic arts field. Ask for it at stores that sell art supplies.)
- Low tack masking tape
- A spoon or bone folder for burnishing (the spoon can no longer be used for food after it has been used for this.)
- Several sheets of blank newspaper to create a soft, slightly padded work surface

Supplies and examples of transferred images

Stroke the release pen on the back of the photocopy.

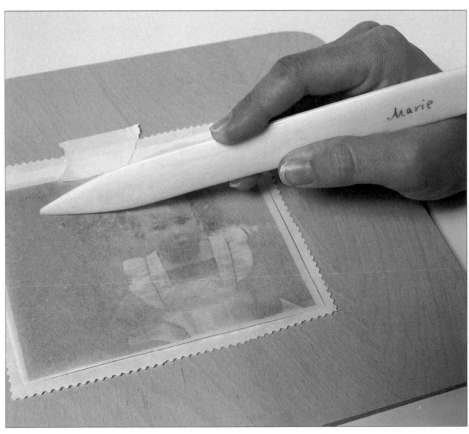

Burnish the print onto the paper.

Here's How

1. Position your photocopied print face down on the paper and secure with a small piece of tape. If you're using thinner paper (like bond paper), turn the paper over and work from the back. You should be able to see the image through the bond paper. If you are using heavier paper (like watercolor paper), work from the front.

2. Starting at the center of the image, stroke the release pen on the paper. You will be able to see the image quite clearly as you stroke – the lacquer makes the paper very transparent. Continue to stroke on the lacquer so it saturates the area you wish to transfer.

3. Immediately after the lacquer has been applied, use the back of a spoon or a bone folder to burnish the back of the paper all over the image area. This helps to release the toner on the photocopy.

4. Carefully turn over the paper and peek under a corner to see if the toner has been released; if not, turn over and repeat steps 2 and 3. Don't be too quick to toss out what looks like a failure. The image will seem a bit blurry and faded at first, but as the lacquer evaporates, it will clear up.

5. After you have successfully transferred the image, let it dry completely (this takes about 30 minutes).

Using the Lacquer Pen on Fabrics

This transfer method also works on some fabrics. The images created on the fabric look like antique cigarette silks of the early 1900s. Use a thick, good quality satin, smooth silk, or a smooth, fine cotton fabric for best results. When working with fabrics, place the fabric, face up, on the work surface. Position the photocopied image, face down, on the fabric and stroke the lacquer pen on the paper to release the toner. Fabrics with this type of transferred image are not washable.

Preserving Memories Under Glass

Mounting photographs between pieces of glass is an impressive technique for creating framed pictures, ornaments, coasters, and refrigerator magnets. You can have a glazier cut the glass pieces for you or you can cut them yourself. Shops that sell supplies for stained glass crafting have all sorts of gorgeous beveled glass pieces and fancy textured and color glass.

You'll Need

- Pieces of 1/8" thick glass cut into rectangle or square shapes to accommodate your photo arrangement (You will need two pieces of glass the same size for each project.)

- Your chosen photograph (a color photocopy is fine)

- Copper foil tape, 1/2" wide (found at shops that sell supplies for making stained glass)

- Craft glue

- Small paint brush

- Large binder clips

Here's How

1. Clean the glass pieces. Be careful to handle them by the edges to prevent fingerprints and smudges.
2. Place one glass piece on your work surface. Position the photograph or photocopy on the glass, using a tiny bit of craft glue to hold it in place. Let the glue dry completely.
3. Carefully place the second piece of glass on top, sandwiching the print between the two glass pieces. Use binder clips on the edges to hold the pieces in place.
4. Measure the circumference of the glass piece and add 1/2". Cut a piece of copper tape this length.

Continued on next page

Gather supplies for preserving memories under glass.

Cut photo or photocopy to the size or shape desired. Add a dab or glue to back of photo to hold it in place on the glass.

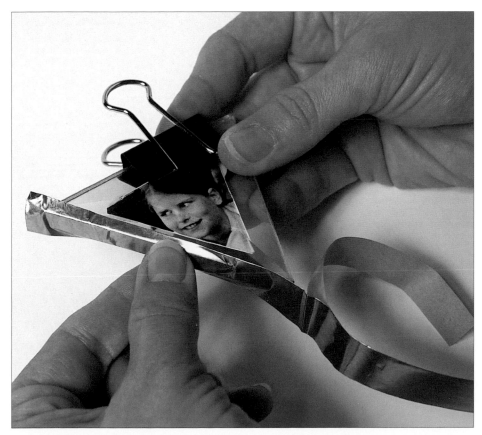

Sandwich the print between the two pieces of glass and use binder clips to hold glass together. Seal edges with copper tape.

Continued from page 26

5. Join the glass pieces together by wrapping the edges of the glass with copper tape. To start, carefully peel back about 3" of the tape's protective paper backing and position the tape on the middle of the glass edge. Press the tape to the edges of the glass, removing the clips and peeling away the backing paper as you go. As you complete each side, fold the edges of the tape over the front and back of the glass. With your fingernail, rub the copper tape firmly to burnish.

PRESERVING MEMORIES UNDER MICA

Mica is a wonderful natural material that is perfect for preserving photographs, pressed flowers, and other memorabilia. Mica is a clear, transparent mineral that is formed in sheets. You can buy it in crafts and lapidary shops. You can split the sheets into layers that will be thinner and lighter in color when separated. (Separating the sheets increases the amount of usable material many times over.) The sheets have a slight amber tint and are not without flaws, as they are a natural material.

Mica sheets can be cut easily with scissors. The layers can be joined with glue, threaded with wire, or taped on the edges with copper foil tape. I use mica sheets for night lights, framed arrangements, and pins and to cover photographs mounted on box tops.

Decorative Paint Techniques to Enhance Your Projects

Decorative paint techniques are easy to do when you have the proper equipment. They can be used to add colorful custom accents to your projects.

STENCILING

Stenciling is a fast and easy way to add lettering and decoration. There are hundreds of pre-cut stencils available in a vast array of motifs. Use a waterbase stencil gel or acrylic paint for stenciling, using very little paint for best results. Stencil brushes or dense sponges work the best to apply the gel or paint.

Here's How

1. Position the stencil on your project and secure with low tack masking tape.
2. Load the paint on your applicator and remove almost all of the paint from the applicator by tapping it on a paper towel.
3. Apply the paint to the project surface through the openings in the stencil.
   - It is best to experiment on a scrap piece of paper before going to your project.
   - If your paint or gel leaks under the stencil, you are using too much!
4. Remove the stencil and let dry. ∞

RUBBER STAMPING

The range of rubber stamps available is huge – there's a stamp available for practically any theme or motif! A set of letters is valuable for adding sayings and personalizing projects. Ink pads come in a vast array of colors, and most inks are acid free. Make sure your ink pad is raised so it can be used with any size of stamp. Practice on a scrap piece of paper before stamping your project.

Here's How

1. Load the stamp evenly with the ink by lightly tapping the stamp on the ink pad.
2. Press the stamp firmly on the surface to transfer ink.
   Don't rock the stamp. Lift the stamp. Let dry. ∞

Stenciling

THERMAL EMBOSSING WITH STAMPS

Thermal embossing uses a stamp, ink, a heat source, and embossing powder to create a raised image on paper. Embossing powders are available in a variety of colors and finishes to create shiny, matte, glittered, or iridescent results.

You'll Need

- A rubber stamp
- A pigment ink pad
- Embossing powder in the color of your choice
- An embossing heat tool or other heat source, such as an iron or toaster oven. (The embossing powder melts at 350 degrees F., so a hair dryer will not work.)

Here's How

1. Stamp your image on your project.
2. While the ink is still wet, sprinkle on the embossing powder to completely cover the image. Shake off excess powder and place back in the jar for later use.
3. *If using an embossing heat tool,* heat the tool and blow hot air on the stamped image for a few seconds. You will see the powder melt. Do not overheat. Let cool. *If using an iron or a toaster oven,* hold the image over the heat source until the powder melts. Be careful not to scorch your project. Let cool. ∞

Rubber Stamping

Varnish Crackling

Varnish Crackling

Crackling is a popular decorative finish that imparts a vintage look. The supplies for creating a crackle finish usually come in a two-part kit that includes a base coat and a top coat. After the crackle finish is dry, antiquing is rubbed over the cracks to emphasize them.

You'll Need

- A crackle finish kit (base coat and top coat)
- Foam brushes
- Decoupage medium
- Clear acrylic sealer (brush-on or spray varnish)
- A photocopied print
- Acrylic glaze (Use a light color of glaze if the background is dark and a dark color if the background is light.)
- A sponge

Here's How

1. Adhere the photocopied print to the surface with decoupage medium. Let dry.
2. Apply a coat of clear acrylic sealer. Let dry.
3. Brush the base coat over the entire project. Let dry completely.
4. Brush on the top coat. Cracks will form immediately.
   - A thin coat will result in fine, small cracks.
   - A thick coat will produce larger cracks.
   Let dry.
5. Thin the acrylic glaze a bit with water. Brush the glaze across the surface. Wipe off the excess with a damp sponge, letting the glaze settle in the cracks. Let dry.
6. Apply a finish coat of clear acrylic sealer. ∞

Flocked Surfaces

Flocking is an old idea that is back. You can see flocked boxes, ornaments, and tables in antique stores. You also see flocking in fine gift stores on the bottoms of coasters and fine placemats.

A flocked surface is soft to the touch like velvet or felt. I find flocking the inside of a shadow box or the bottom of a coaster gives a rich, textured look that is professional-looking. It's also a practical way to protect fine furniture. Flocking comes in a variety of rich colors. One kit can cover a large area.

You'll Need

- A flocking kit in the color of your choice (The kit comes with colored adhesive and flocking fibers.)
- Acrylic craft paint that matches the color of the flocking
- Freezer paper
- Foam brushes

Here's How

1. Protect your work surface with freezer paper.
2. Paint the surface to be flocked with acrylic craft paint. Let dry completely.
3. Brush on a coat of the flocking adhesive.
4. Working quickly, before the adhesive dries, apply the flocking fibers. (They come in a plastic bottle that you "poof" over the wet adhesive by squeezing the fibers out of the bottle in small bursts.) Apply a thick layer of the flocking for an even and complete coverage. Do not tap the surface or shake off excess fibers now. Let dry overnight.
5. Tap the excess fibers off the surface on to a piece of freezer paper. Place the fibers back in the bottle for later use.

Flocked Surfaces

Natural Accents – Preserving Flowers

Many important occasions in our lives come with flowers. We give flowers when we fall in love, when we marry, when our children are born, to celebrate anniversaries and birthdays, and to remember our loved ones when they leave us. I like to preserve special flowers by pressing or air drying them.

The best dried flowers come from perfect, fresh specimens. As it's not always possible to immediately dry flowers given for a special occasion, do the best you can. (You can always remove a blossom or two from an arrangement and preserve them.) If you wait until the flowers are fully open and starting to wilt, the results will be disappointing.

AIR DRYING FLOWERS

You'll Need

- Flowers (Some blossoms that dry well using this method are roses, lavender, delphinium, asters, dahlias, and carnations.)
- Wire coat hangers
- Rubber bands
- Labels for recording the occasion, the recipient, and the giver

Here's How

1. Strip off the leaves at the bottom of the stem where the stem will be bound. This increases the strength of the stems and speeds the drying time. Leaves on flower stems can become brittle when dried, so leave just a few.
2. Gather up a small bunch of stems with flowers. Be sure they are not so bunched up that air can't circulate and secure the stem ends with a rubber band.
3. Attach the bound bunch to a wire coat hanger, using the rubber band. This technique is quick and holds the bunch while it dries. If you use string or raffia to hold the flowers, your flowers and leaves will end up all over the floor because the stems shrink as they dry, but a rubber band will hold the bunch tight during the whole drying process.
4. Slip a paper label on each hanger to identify each bunch of flowers.
5. Hang your completed hangers in a dark, dry, well-ventilated room away from direct sunlight until completely dry – generally two to three weeks.

PRESSING FLOWERS AND FOLIAGE

Pressing is a simple method of preserving flowers and foliage. The two-dimensional products are suitable for photocopying, for displaying in potpourri or under glass, and for mounting on cards and labels. You can purchase a flower press or microwave press or use a large book to press your plant materials. (You also can purchase pressed flowers and leaves for your projects, but they are never as nice or as varied as plants that you press yourself, and they won't have the same associations or memories.)

Pressing flowers and foliage takes, on average, three to four weeks. Press your flowers while the blooms are still fresh. If you wait too long, the flowers will dry brown and the results will be disappointing.

USING A PURCHASED FLOWER PRESS OR A BOOK

You'll Need

- Flowers (Flowers suitable for pressing include hydrangea, pansy, lobelia, forget-me-nots, ferns, larkspur, delphinium, violets, and wild roses.)
- Absorbent paper
- A flower press or large, heavy book
- Envelopes for storing
- *For pressing flowers with bulky stamens,* thin polyester batting

Here's How

1. *If you're using a press,* place the plants between two absorbent, smooth sheets and place in the press. Place flowers with bulky stamens between two sheets of thin polyester batting and then place between the absorbent sheets. *If you are using a book,* place two sheets of absorbent paper between the pages to protect the book and place the flowers between the sheets.
2. Check the press in about two weeks. Drying times vary for different flowers. You cannot harm the flowers by leaving them in the press after they have dried, but you can damage them if you remove them before the drying process is complete.
3. Store the pressed plants flat in labeled envelopes.

MICROWAVE PRESSING

Microwave pressing allows you to create pressed flowers almost instantly. I found color retention with a microwave press was excellent. I also was able to press thick, fleshy flowers that would be difficult to press with a standard press. The ease and quality of the pressed specimens outweighed the expense of the press.

Flowers that have been pressed

Storing pressed flowers for future use.

Preserving Memory Projects

Memorabilia and photographs can be used to make wonderful gifts and memorable packaging, holiday ornaments, decorative home accessories, and wearables. In the pages that follow, you'll see a variety of examples that I hope will inspire you to create projects with your photos and keepsakes that your family will treasure. Refer to the step-by-step instructions in the Techniques section for detailed information on specific processes, procedures, and supplies. Enjoy!

Boxes & Albums for Photos & Memories

Wooden boxes that are designed to hold memorabilia can be attractive enough to place in the family room so everyone can have access to them. They can be stacked in a bookshelf, or smaller boxes that hold a stack of recent photos can add a functional accent to a coffee table. You can label the boxes by year or event or assign a box to each family member for his or her favorite photographs. The designs are simple and the decorating techniques easy, so the whole family can help create them. Line the boxes with archival tissue paper to help preserve the contents.

WOODEN PHOTO STORAGE BOXES

You'll Need

- Wooden boxes that measure 9" x 12" x 5" with sliding tops
- Acrylic wood stain or glaze or acrylic craft paint
- Photocopies of favorite photographs
- Decoupage medium
- 1" foam brushes
- Acrylic matte varnish or spray sealer
- Computer generated or hand lettered labels
- *For the photo frame:* 2 ft. of 1/4" balsa wood to make a frame, white craft glue, archival (acid free) tissue paper

Here's How

1. I wanted the wood grain of these boxes to show, so I stained them with an acrylic glaze. Do not paint or stain the insides of the boxes unless your paint or stain is acid free. Let the boxes dry completely.
2. Decoupage a print on the lid (as shown on the Family Storage Box) or create a collage of motifs from a special event (as shown on the Vacation Memories Box).
3. Decoupage a label on the end of each box.
4. Seal with spray varnish.

To make the frame for the Family Storage Box:
1. Cut pieces of balsa wood to fit the photo.
2. Stain the wood pieces to match the box. Let dry.
3. Glue the frame in place with white craft glue. ᎒

VACATIONS
1996

BROWNING
est. 1984

FAMILY HEIRLOOMS PHOTO BOX

You'll Need

- Papier mache box with rusty tin lid, 7" x 5" x 2-3/4"
- Acrylic craft paint
- Metallic gold paint
- Photocopy of a favorite photograph
- Decoupage medium
- 1" foam brushes
- Acrylic matte varnish or spray sealer
- Hand lettered label
- White craft glue
- *Optional extras:* 2 ft. of 1/4" balsa wood to make a frame, white craft glue, a piece of mica as large as the photocopied photo, small silk flowers to coordinate with paint color, archival (acid free) tissue paper

Here's How

1. Paint the box base with acrylic craft paint. Do not paint the inside of the box unless your paint is acid free. Let dry completely.
2. Decoupage the photocopied photo on the lid.
3. Decoupage a label on the end of the box.
4. Seal with spray varnish. Let dry.
5. Cut pieces of balsa wood to fit around the photo.
6. Paint the wood pieces with metallic gold paint. Let dry.
7. Place a piece of mica on top of the photo.
8. Glue the frame pieces in place with white craft glue.
9. Glue silk flowers around the frame.
10. Line the box with archival tissue paper to protect the contents. ∾

PHOTO ALBUMS

*Wooden album covers are a wonderful surface to showcase treasures.
The albums come complete with hardware. The covers were created
with decoupaged photocopies and a variety of decorative accents.*

Here's How

Step One: Covering the Surface

The wooden album pieces are covered completely with decorative paper adhered with decoupage medium. On the large album, the paper was folded over the edges and glued on the inside. On the small album, a pencil wrapped with sandpaper was used to sand the cover paper flush with the decorative scalloped edge.

Step Two: Decorative Decoupaging

The large album was decoupaged with torn pieces of pages photocopied from an old journal and a copy of an old sepia toned photograph of my Grandmama Provan. The pages were from a book Grandmama kept to learn the English language as she traveled to Canada from France to marry my grandfather.

The smaller album features an all over decoupage of a photocopied cradle roll certificate, photocopied hand-tinted photos, and photocopied pressed flowers.

Additional coats of decoupage medium were applied to the surfaces.

Step Three: Adding Accents

When the decoupage medium was completely dry, both albums were accented with rub-on gold leaves and gold lettering.

Metal accents glued on the larger album include a lacy oval frame, a rose garland, and a bird charm. The smaller album has a matching ribbon page marker adorned with a small gold charm.

Step Four: Finishing Touches

Two coats of matte acrylic varnish were brushed on the surfaces to protect the decoupaged designs. After the varnish was dry, the albums were assembled. ๑

Pictured from left: Grandmama Provan's Memories Album, Treasured Memories Album

Using Memories in Home Decor

The home decor projects in this section illustrate creative and beautiful ways to decorate with treasured photographs and memorabilia, including decorative plates, a Seaside Vacation Wreath, and a silk flower arrangement constructed on an old open book. More utilitarian objects include a collage tray, coasters, switch plates, trivets, and clay pots. Use the project photographs and instructions as inspirations for creating decorative items with your family photos.

DECORATIVE PHOTO PLATES

These bread and butter plates and the saucer shown here are adorned with charms, seashells, and a baby's bracelet. Other options are rubber stamps, decoupage, painted accents, and stenciling.

You'll Need

- Color photocopy of photograph (cut with circle cutter into 4-1/2" circle or to size needed for plate you are using)
- White ceramic plate, 7" diameter used here
- Glue stick (a permanent glue stick works best)
- Permanent markers to add sayings
- Thin white glue
- Two-part pour-on resin coating

Here's How

See "Using a Two-Part Resin Coating" in the Techniques section.

1. Glue the photocopy in the center of the plate with the glue stick. Let dry completely.
2. Brush the photocopy with a coat of white glue to seal the image. Let dry until completely clear. (This step can be omitted if the image is an actual photograph or was printed on photographic paper.)
3. Decorate the rim of the plate. I used a baby bracelet and colored plastic charms for the Baby Victoria Plate, plastic softball charms and stars for the Hampton All Stars Plate, and seashells and an anchor charm for the Beach Plate – all attached with white craft glue. Let glue dry.
4. With a permanent pen, add a saying.
5. Following the resin finish manufacturer's directions, mix 1 oz. of resin coating (equal amounts of resin and hardener) and pour into the well of the plate. Swirl the plate to evenly coat and seal the image. (This action will also give you an even edge.)
6. De-gas the bubbles. Place in a dust free area until resin is set. When finished, display your plate proudly. ∽

Antique Little Girl Saucer

A saucer (5" diameter) with a scalloped edge from a thrift store was used for the small plate. The photo was edged with tiny beads and the plate was decorated with antique buttons and beads. Some white silk rosebuds were glued on after the coating was dry. ∽

Hampton Park All Stars

Katelyn Louise · May 19 · 1995 · 7 lbs · 8oz · Victoria... God of hand the from blown Stardust of bits are Babies

BABY KATIE

We remember moments We remember days We do not remember days

Grandmas are just antique Little Girls

WEBSTER Queens

41

Seaside Memory & Vacation Wreath

Here's How

Step One: Creating the Memory Bubbles

1. Decoupage photocopies of vacation photos on different sizes of wooden discs.
2. Sand the edges to trim off the excess paper and seal with a coat of white glue. Let dry.
3. Paint the edges with acrylic paint. Let dry.
4. For a high gloss finish, pour on a resin coating. Let dry.

Step Two: Wrapping the Wreath

1. A 12" straw wreath was wrapped with two yards of twisted rope. Both ends of the rope were glued to the back of the wreath to secure.
2. Dark green colored wood excelsior was mixed with a thin bodied white craft glue and draped on the wrapped wreath form.
3. Because shells are heavy, I also used a generous amount of hot glue to adhere the excelsior base firmly to the wreath form.
4. A natural colored net-like ribbon was woven in and around the center of the wreath and glued in place.

Step Three: Decorating and Finishing

1. The collected shells and memory bubbles were hot glued to the wreath in a cluster on the bottom.
2. To finish the wreath and ready it for display, add a wire hanger to the back.

Vintage Open Book Arrangement

This arrangement inspires sweet memories of yesteryear and is an elegant accent for a romantic boudoir or a front entrance table. It started out with an old book found at a thrift store for 25 cents. Because the arrangement is glued directly into the book, I don't advise using a family heirloom or a valuable edition. The photocopied photo of my mom was hand colored. The colors of the silk flowers, ribbons, and small crocheted doilies echo the colors in the photo.

Here's How

Step One: Preparing the Book Base

1. With the book closed, paint the edges of the pages with gold metallic acrylic craft paint. Open the book to let dry so the pages do not stick together.
2. Wrap 1 yd. of ribbon around the open book like a parcel. I also removed an inscription from the inside cover of the book and glued it on the open page.
3. To give the book a little height and to tip it forward a bit, glue the book on a 6" square wooden plaque base with two wooden knobs glued on the bottom at the back.

Step Two: Building the Arrangement

1. A florist anchor was glued in the middle of the open book.
2. A 3" cube of floral foam (the kind made for dried flowers) was pushed on the anchor.
3. Moss was pinned to the floral foam to form the base for the arrangement.
4. A hand-tinted photocopy of a photograph in an oval metal frame was glued on the base. The photo forms the focal point of the arrangement.
5. Silk flowers and leaves were arranged and glued around the framed photo. Dried flowers also could be used.

Step Three: Adding Accents

Accents include small crocheted doilies, a small handmade teddy bear, and a copy of an antique calling card. Pressed tin corner accents were bent to hold the calling card and clipped on the bottom of the open book. A multi-loop bow of wire-edge tulle was added to the back of the arrangement to finish. ∾

THREE-PANEL DESK SCREEN

A wooden triptych can be used to make a desk screen that would also be wonderful on a writing desk or the guest book table at a wedding or anniversary celebration. The triptych panels were taped off with 1" wide masking tape, then painted to form the stripes. After the tape was removed, the whole surface was washed with a white glaze. An assortment of small metal frames and corner pieces were antiqued with white craft paint. Photographs were photocopied and reduced to fit the frames. Wire-edge ribbon, 1/4" wide, was used to make the bows that were glued to the panels behind the pictures. Use a gold calligraphy paint pen to add the names and date.

Scott

Marie

December 1984

DESK PAD AND PEN HOLDER

A wooden plaque makes a practical desk message center for the office and is a wonderful idea for a Father's Day gift!

Here's How

Step One: Staining

Stain the plaque with dark brown acrylic glaze. Let dry.

Step Two: Decoupaging

Adhere the enlarged photocopy with decoupage medium. Let dry. Sand edges of the paper flush with the plaque.

Step Three: Sealing and Gluing Accents

Seal with two coats of white glue. A mountable pen, purchased at a craft store, is glued to the plaque. I used white craft glue to glue pebbles around the pen base.

Step Four: Applying Coating

Coat the pebbles and the top of the plaque with two-part pour-on resin.

Step Five: Finishing

When the resin is fully set, remove the backing paper from a 3" x 5" sticky note pad and affix to the top. Flock the bottom of the plaque and add the date and place with a gold paint pen. ∾

FLOWER FACES ON CLAY POTS

Fanciful vases made from inexpensive clay pots decorated with photos, flora, and fauna and filled with fresh flowers or a potted plant are a welcome gift. The pour-on resin coating is completely watertight when set. Ideas for designs include placing wings on baby photos to create cute and whimsical "butterfly babies." Or cut children's faces from photos and place them in the centers of pressed flowers. You also can create wonder and charm when you change the scale of the surrounding motifs as I did for the small yellow pot, where the children sit on gigantic ivy leaves, making them appear to be gnomes and fairies.

You'll Need

- Clay pot
- Pour-on resin coating
- Photocopies of photographs and floral motifs and/or cutouts from wrapping paper
- Acrylic craft paint for base painting
- Foam brushes
- White glue
- Masking tape
- Large plastic bottle that the clay pot will fit over to keep the pot off your work surface as your pour the resin coating
- Medium grade sandpaper
- *Optional:* Decoupage medium

Here's How

1. Paint the outside of the pot with acrylic paint, if you wish. Let dry.
2. Decoupage photocopied motifs on the pot with white glue or decoupage medium. Let dry.
3. Seal the motifs with a coat of white glue.
4. Place a piece of masking tape over the drainage hole on the inside of the pot.
5. Place the pot upside down over the plastic bottle.
6. Following manufacturer's instructions, mix 1 oz. of resin coating (equal amounts of resin and hardener) and pour over the pot. Brush the resin over the outside of the pot to evenly coat and seal it. Let the excess resin drip on the protected work space.
7. De-gas the bubbles and place in a dust free area to set for 12 hours.
8. Remove the masking tape. Mix another 1 oz. of resin coating. Pour into the pot and brush up to the top edge to completely coat the inside. Set the pot down, right side up. De-gas bubbles and set aside for 72 hours.
9. Sand any drips from the top of the pot with medium grade sandpaper. ∞

STACKABLE BLOCKS

Wooden blocks of various sizes make an engaging photo gallery when decorated with hand-tinted photocopies and stenciled motifs.

Here's How

Step One: Base Painting
Base paint the blocks with acrylic craft paints.

Step Two: Decoupaging
Decoupage black and white photocopies on the sides of the blocks.

Step Three: Tinting Photos
Seal the photocopies with matte varnish. Let dry. Use the Tint O' Pauge method to hand color the photos.

Step Four: Adding Accents
Stencil letters and decorative motifs with gold metallic paint. Let dry. Finish on all sides with a coat of matte varnish. ∾

BABY DOOR SIGN

Every household with a new baby needs this thoughtful gift! A wooden door sign is stained brown with an acrylic glaze before the photocopy is decoupaged in place. Lettering is added with an alphabet stencil, and when dry, outlined with a black permanent marker so the letters are clearly visible. ∾

SLEEPING ELVES NIGHT LIGHT

This personalized night light was created with mica sheets and a photocopy on transparent film. The photocopy was trimmed right to the motif and floated in between the mica layers, which were glued together. It was easy to pop off the plastic cover on a purchased night light and glue the mica one in place with silicone glue. ❧

LIGHT SWITCH PLATES

Switch plates covered with photocopied photos light up any room into little bits of family history. Choose photos that can work around the switch and the screw holes. Use decoupage medium to adhere the photocopies and, when the decoupage medium has dried, sand the edges flush for a perfect fit. Or tear the edges of the paper for a different look. Painted charms and a painted border can be added. Coat the prints with two coats of white glue and when dry, apply a two-part pour-on resin coating for a practical, easy to clean surface. ❧

Trays and Coasters

Photographs displayed on trays and coasters make practical, useful gifts that remind us of special moments. The resin coatings make them easy to care for, and the flocking on the bottom of the coasters protects fine furniture and adds a professional finishing touch.

STACK OF COASTERS

Small wooden plaques make wonderful coasters to commemorate special events like weddings and are a thoughtful housewarming gift for newlyweds. The black and white photocopies were very lightly hand-tinted. The edges of the plaques (4" square) were painted with dark maroon paint, then silver paint and were lightly sanded for a distressed look. The tops of the coasters received a two-part pour-on resin coating. The bottoms were flocked with a dark maroon flocking. I used a matching maroon ribbon to tie them together. ∾

COLLAGE TRAY

This wooden tray is decorated with a decoupage photo mosaic technique and sealed with a resin coating.

Here's How

Step One: Making Copies and Cutting

1. Photocopy photographs and old letters, enlarging or reducing as needed.
2. Cut photocopies into 2" squares with a paper cutter.

Step Two: Arranging and Decoupaging

1. Arrange the pieces on the tray. I experimented a bit and moved the pieces around, trying different combinations to create an interesting composition and to mix the colors.
2. Adhere the pieces on the tray with decoupage medium. Let dry.
3. Seal with a coat of white glue. Let dry. Apply a second coat of white glue. Let dry.

Step Three: Applying the Resin Coating

Finish the tray by applying a two-part resin pour-on coating. ∞

Coaster Tray

This useful tray is a photo gallery of a treasured holiday in Holland. The photocopies were printed in blue and purple monotones and decoupaged on the coaster pieces, then crackled to give the look of old Delft tiles. The bottom of the tray sports an enlargement of a postcard in the blue monotone. After all the decoupaged motifs were sealed with white glue, the top surface of the tray and the coasters were coated with a pour-on resin. The bottom of each coaster was flocked with warm white flocking. Porcelain drawer pulls, bought at the hardware store, were affixed to the tray for handles. ❧

TILE TRIVET

A plain white tile takes on a new look with decoupage, crackling, and a pour-on resin coating and becomes a commemorative trivet. Its large size (8" square) makes it possible to create an artistic, thoughtful arrangement.

You'll Need

- Wooden trivet frame and plain tile
- Photocopies of photographs and memorabilia and/or motifs cut from wrapping paper
- Decoupage medium
- Pour-on resin coating
- Foam brushes
- Thin white glue
- Supplies for hand coloring photos
- Scissors for cutting motifs
- Crackle medium
- Glaze for antiquing the crackling

Here's How

1. Gather an assortment of photos and objects and make copies. Here I used portrait photos, buttons, a key, fragments of sheet music, a frame, a signature, and drawings of violins. Hand color some of the photos.
2. Cut out the motifs. I used decorative edge scissors to cut out some items, and small scissors and a craft knife for others. The sheet music pieces have torn edges.
3. Arrange them on the tile, trying different configurations until you're pleased with the result.
4. Adhere the cutouts to the tile with decoupage medium. Let dry.
5. Apply one to two additional coats of decoupage medium. Let dry.
6. Apply crackle basecoat. Let dry.
7. Apply crackle topcoat. Cracks will form. Let dry.
8. Rub glaze over the cracks to highlight them. Use the same glaze to stain the wooden trivet frame. Let dry.
9. Seal the design with a coat of white craft glue. Let dry.
10. Apply the pour-on resin coating. Let dry.
11. Place the tile in the frame. ❧

Framing & Displaying Photos

A frame makes any photo look special. Examples include simple frames decorated with photos and drawings, shadow boxes to hold collages of memorabilia, photos under glass and on canvas, and decorative frames made from polymer clay.

SEASIDE MEMORY FRAME

The frame that accents your photograph can also be a canvas to showcase memories. Here, the photograph of Michelle searching for shells on the beach is framed with a photocopy of a photo of the same beach.

You'll Need

- Wooden frame
- 2 Photocopies of related photographs
- Decoupage medium
- Foam brush
- Sandpaper
- Thin white glue
- Scissors for cutting motifs
- Acrylic varnish
- Shells or other memorabilia

Here's How

1. The photocopy was enlarged to fit the frame. Photo was trimmed to fit frame and decoupaged in place. The edges were sanded flush to the edge of the frame for a clean finish.
2. Some of the shells Michelle collected were glued to the frame with white craft glue.
3. When dry, two coats of acrylic satin varnish were applied.
4. Photo of Michelle was taped to back of frame. ∾

WOODEN FRAME FOR DAD

Children's drawings are art in its purest form, and this drawing by our daughter Katie of her dad is probably the best likeness of my husband that I have ever seen! The simple wooden frame was painted with acrylic craft paint in colors that match the drawing. The drawing was photocopied and reduced, then decoupaged in place. Lettering was added, using a felt pen with slow drying ink that was thermal embossed with copper embossing powder. A finishing coat of acrylic satin varnish was added to protect the frame before proudly hanging it for display. ∾

3-D Decoupage Photos

*In these pictures, the main motifs are cut from
a second copy of the print and attached for a
three-dimensional effect. This decoupage technique
is easy to do with a minimum of equipment.*

You'll Need

- Two photocopies of a favorite photograph (Choose a photograph with a subject that will be easy to cut out, one that doesn't have a lot of detail.)
- Matte laminating sheets (found at stationery stores, office supply stores, and craft stores)
- Card stock paper, in a dark color
- Piece of wood cut 1/4" larger all around than the background photograph
- Acrylic craft paint to match photo
- Sandpaper
- Acrylic varnish
- Double-sided foam tape or pop-up dots (sold at rubber stamp and craft stores)
- Small, sharp scissors
- Glue stick
- White craft glue

Here's How

1. Sand wood piece. Paint with acrylic craft paint. Let dry. Varnish. Let dry.
2. Glue both photocopies to card stock with the glue stick. (This makes the photocopies stronger and more rigid.)
3. Laminate both photocopies with matte laminate sheets. To start, carefully peel back the backing paper and adhere at one end of the photocopy. Cover the photocopies with the laminate, smoothing the laminate as you peel back the paper. Burnish down with your fingers to smooth and remove any bubbles. Work slowly and carefully – if you get wrinkles, you can't pull up the laminate and start over. *Option:* Have the photos laminated at a shop that has a laminating machine.
4. Trim one laminated photocopy to fit the painted wood piece. Cut out the main motif from the other print. The better your cutting job, the more successful your project will be.
5. Place small pieces of foam tape all over the back of the cutout motif, spacing the tape pieces about 1/2" apart to give the print the stability it needs to lay straight. Place the cutout on the background print.
6. Glue the background print to the wooden base with white craft glue. ∞

These photos are displayed with some creative easel ideas. A store-bought teddy holds the photo of Katie and her teddy, and an easel fashioned from a piece of driftwood with shells glued on top holds the seaside photograph.

MEMORY SHADOW BOXES

Shadow boxes are a wonderful way to showcase photographs with treasured souvenirs that won't fit in an album. These sentimental showcases begin with a theme or a person and some plain wooden boxes. Use them as ideas for displaying your own cherished pieces.

Uncle Al's Memory Box includes a branch, glycerine treated oak leaves, framed photographs of Uncle Al as a child and a graduate, a photocopy of a certificate, a letter opener, and some wooden acorns. The objects were mounted at different levels by gluing the pieces on wooden risers. An old key is glued to the outside corner of the box to help bring the arrangement forward. The box would fit nicely in a gentlemen's den.

The Sports Theme Shadow Box feature medals, collected pins, events tickets, and event credentials. The credentials were photocopied, then laminated to look like the originals.

The event tickets were reduced to fit into the arrangement. It would look great in a family room or game room.

Tips

- Select pieces that amplify and enhance the theme.
- Paint the box in colors that coordinate with the colors of your theme.
- Flock the inside of the box to create a rich, professional looking background to show off your display.
- Make a frame from pieces of wooden decorative molding cut to size and glued on the rim of the box. ✑

PHOTOS UNDER GLASS

Photos framed in glass can float with dried flowers, pieces of lace, antique letters, and other flat, two-dimensional memory pieces. Follow the general instructions for "Preserving Memories Under Glass" to create your own personalized frames. The examples on this page were made with pieces of beveled glass. Using ribbons in coordinating colors to hang the frames creates a unified wall display.

Glass Pictures to Hang

(shown here at right)

Keep these small so they are not too heavy. A good size is 3" x 5". For the hangers, you will need 19 gauge brass wire. Cut a piece of wire 8" long and make loops for threading through ribbon or cord for hanging. Bend the wire so that it rests on the top of the finished glass picture. Use a strong jewelry glue to glue the wire hanger to the top. Let the glue dry completely. Use small pieces of copper tape to tape where the hanger meets the picture for extra strength.

Picture with Pressed Flowers

(shown on page 73)

A beveled glass frame shows a photo of Grandma and Grandpa Arscott surrounded by pressed flowers.

Position a photograph or a collage of photos on one piece of glass and arrange pressed flowers around it. Tickets, pieces of lace, letter fragments, and other memorabilia can be added. Use little dots of glue to hold everything in place. Place the second piece of glass on top and tape the edges with copper tape. Display the finished picture on a small easel or on a shelf with a plate rail. *Option:* Create your arrangement on a piece of mat board and place a piece of glass cut to the same dimensions on top. Secure the edges with copper tape.

PHOTOS ON CANVAS

These photographs have been decoupaged on artist's stretched canvas. Brass tacks adorn the sides. The surfaces are crackled and antiqued to give the feeling of a classical masterpiece starring your loved ones.

You'll Need

- Pre-stretched artist's canvas, 5" x 7" or a 8" x 10" (available at fine art stores and large craft outlets)
- Photocopy of your favorite photograph to fit the canvas
- Decoupage medium
- 1" foam brush
- Brass tacks
- Acrylic craft paint in one dark color and one light color
- Paint brushes
- Crackle medium
- Acrylic varnish
- Household sponge
- Tack hammer

Here's How

1. Tear the edges of your photocopy. Glue to canvas with decoupage medium. Let dry.
2. Apply crackle basecoat. Let dry completely.
3. Apply crackle topcoat. Cracks will form. Let dry completely.
4. Thin acrylic paint with water and wash over the entire canvas, avoiding the faces in the print. Wipe back excess paint on the surface with a damp sponge. Use both light and dark washes so the crackles show up all over the print.
5. With full strength paint, paint the edges of the canvas. Use a dry brush method as you approach the main elements of the print. Let dry.
6. Brush on a coat of acrylic varnish.
7. Hammer the tacks into the sides of the canvas about 1" apart. ෨

Polymer Clay Frames

With polymer clay, you can create personalized frames that are uniquely yours. The process is simple: roll out the clay, impress it with found objects, leaves, or rubber stamps, bake it in your home oven, and add painted details. The clay also can be used to make pebble easels to hold your frames.

You'll Need

- Polymer clay in light colors such as white, cream, or beige – one 2 oz. block for each frame (For the Rock Slab Frame, use transparent clay.)
- Glazed tile (I use a tile for a work surface – it goes right into the oven for baking.)
- Hard acrylic roll brayer
- Polymer clay cutting blade or craft knife
- Found natural materials, such as leaves, shells, and twigs
- Shape templates: ovals, circles, and squares
- Alphabet rubber stamp set to personalize your frame with names or sayings
- Acrylic paint
- Paint brushes
- Clear acrylic varnish
- *For the Rock Slab Frame,* you need a variety of kitchen herbs and spices. My favorites include poppy seeds, chili spice, poultry seasoning, and pepper.

Here's How

1. Condition the clay well. For the Rock Slab Frame, mix 1 tsp. of kitchen spice per ounce into transparent clay.
2. Roll the clay 1/4" thick to the size you wish. You can create up to a 6" square frame with one 2 oz. block of clay.
3. Trim the edges with a blade or leave them uneven.
4. Using a shape template, cut out the opening for the photograph.
5. Decorate the frame by pressing in found objects or personalizing with alphabet rubber stamps.
6. Bake frame according to manufacturer's instructions. Let cool.
7. Paint impressions on the frame with acrylic paint thinned with a bit of water. Use washes of color and wipe off the excess paint to reveal the details of the leaves and other objects. Accent lettering by stippling on a dark acrylic color and wiping off the excess around the letters. Touch up the lettering as needed with a fine brush. Let dry.
8. Finish with a coat of clear acrylic varnish. ∞

Pebble Easels

Pebble easels are special stones that you can make to hold your frames. Make them from transparent clay mixed with kitchen spices. Roll a piece of clay in the palm of your hand into a pebble shape. Press a piece of thin card stock in the center of the pebble to form a slit for the frame to sit in. Paint and bake according to manufacturer's instructions. Finish with clear acrylic varnish. ∞

VOTIVE CANDLE LAMPS

This glowing photo lantern diffuses the flicker of a votive candle to display a collection of memories. If you don't have four coordinating photographs, you can repeat a selection on two sides or all four sides or use colored vellum on some panels.

You'll Need

- 4 Photos that have been photocopied to vellum or clear film, minimum 4" x 6"
- 1/4" balsa wood strips
- Short pins
- Brass tacks
- Tacky craft glue
- Silicone glue

Here's How

1. Building the Frame. The simple rectangular framework is constructed from 1/4" balsa wood strips. You'll need four pieces 6" long and eight pieces 4" long. Use glue and short pins to construct the framework. See diagram for construction of frame.
2. Attaching the Photos. The photographs can be photocopied on vellum or clear film. Trim the prints to 4" x 6". Affix the vellum panels to the frame with silicone base glue or double sided tape. **Do not** use water based glue – it wrinkles vellum.
3. Decorate the corners with small brass tacks. ✑

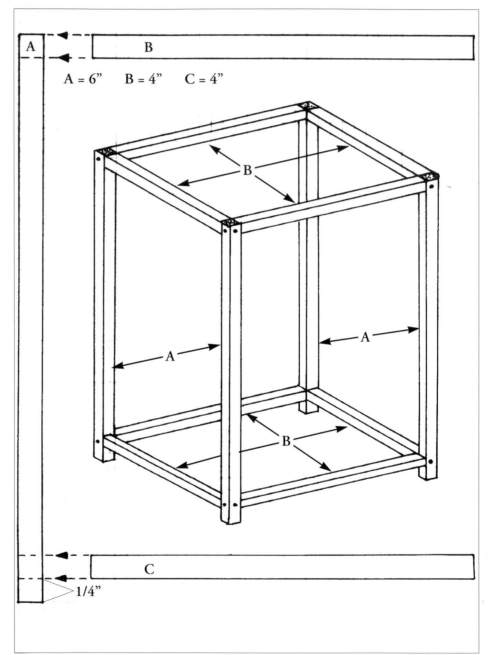

A = 6"   B = 4"   C = 4"

MAGNETS

Use your photos to decorate magnets for your refrigerator or filing cabinet. It's easy!

- **For wooden disc magnets,** decoupage prints on wooden discs, paint the edges with acrylic craft paint, and apply a pour-on resin coating. Add words or dates with a permanent marker. Press strips of magnetic tape on the back.

- **For glass magnets,** arrange photos and dried flowers on a piece of mat board 2-1/2" square, top with glass cut to the same size, and seal the edges with copper tape. Add a 2" strip of self-adhesive magnet tape to the back. ∾

MEMORY CANDLES

*Memory candles make a lovely commemorative gift. For complete instructions,
see "Using Photos on Candles." Try using decorative edge scissors to trim the photos and
different types of paper for lettering.* ∾

Calendars

Calendars are marvelous memory crafting projects because they hold an abbreviated account of your busy life, and they are wonderful gifts for family and friends. Make it a tradition in your home during the New Year's holiday to review the old year's calendar and make a new one together as a family. I save all my old calendars and find them useful to help me recall dates and events. Many copy shops will create a full size calendar from your photographs.

SCHOOL DAYS CALENDAR

This calendar was designed to keep track of children's school events. Any family member may mark special events, important days, and school meetings to keep the household organized.

You'll Need

- Wooden calendar (I used a pre-cut model, but you can substitute pieces of thin plywood, one 14" x 18" and one 2" x 13", and purchased calendar pages.)
- Acrylic craft paint (black, red, green, metallic gold, white, brown, yellow, terra cotta)
- Paint brushes
- Photocopies of school photos
- Wooden shapes (apples, stars, schoolhouse, plus letters and numbers)
- Alphabet stencil with letters 5/8" high
- White craft glue
- Decoupage medium
- 1" foam brush
- Masking tape
- 2 yds. jute string
- Clear acrylic varnish
- Masking tape

Here's How

Paint:
1. Mask off a 1/2" border all around the base of the calendar. Paint the inside area with black acrylic paint.
2. Paint the accent pieces with acrylic paint.
3. Cut the wooden piece that holds the calendar pages on the board to a point at one end.
4. Paint the piece so it looks like a pencil.
5. Stencil "School Days" with black acrylic paint. Let dry.

Decorate and Assemble:
1. Decoupage the photos in place with decoupage medium.
2. Glue all the wooden accents in place with the white craft glue. Let dry.
3. Varnish all wood pieces with clear acrylic varnish.
4. Arrange the calendar pages and top with the pencil piece. Tie in place with jute string. ∽

ABC 123

Brentwood

SCHOOL DAYS

April 1999	Sunday	Monday	Tuesday	Wednesday	Thursday	Friday	Saturday
April 6 - Teacher Interviews mrs. ma 4:30pm mrs. Evans 6 pm						1	2 / LAX 3
Tuesday - Katie Dance 5:15 to 6:15	4	5	Parent Teacher Interviews 6	BBall 7	Katie: Year Book meeting 8	9	LAX 10
Wednesday - BBall for Katie and Lena	11	12	13	Lena's field trip to IMAX BBall 14	Jonathan's field trip to museum 15	16	LAX
Jonathan - Lacrosse Practice Sat. Afternoons	18	Pro-Day No school 19	20	BBall 21	22	23	LAX
	25	26	27	Hot dog Day BBall 28	29		

APPLE

IMAGE TRANSFER CALENDAR

Rubber stamp stores, craft stores, and memory crafting outlets have remarkable kits and surfaces for creating your own calendar art.
For this calendar, I found a wonderful calendar pad that was easy to work with. To create the image transfers, I used color photocopies and a lacquer pen. A rubber stamp set made easy work of the blocks. Rubber number and alphabet stamps can be used for dates and months, or they can be hand lettered. I added an inspirational saying to each page with a permanent black marker. By keeping the lettering simple and whimsical, anyone can do the printing.

Here's How

Step One: Transferring Images

Make color photocopies and transfer images. (See "Paper Image Transferring" in the Techniques section.) I used children's photos and flowers.

Step Two: Stamping and Lettering

Using a black stamp pad, stamp the square blocks. Letter the months and the days. Add sayings if you like. I made the calendar perpetual by not adding the days of the week. With birthdays and anniversaries printed in, it's a perfect gift for family. ∽

May

1	2	3	4	5
6	7	8	9	
10	11	12	13	14
15	16	17	18 Katie's B.D.	
19	20	21	22	
23	24	25	26	27
28	29			
30	31			

August

February

April

Bloom where
you are
Planted

Fabric Memories

PILLOWS

Decorator pillows adorned with family treasures and photographs are another way to preserve the past and celebrate it every day. Special cherished items and photographs can be displayed and framed with decorative braid and stitching. Photographs can be transferred to plain, light colored cotton fabric using transfer medium or iron-on transfer paper.

The pillow covers are made of embossed felt and brushed felt, which is available in a wide range of decorator colors. On felt, it's easy to cut out decorative openings that don't require hemming.

Dusty Rose Treasure Pillow

This pillow has a panel of soft gauzy fabric that with machine stitching, forms a grid to cover buttons, old jewelry pieces, beads, and ribbon roses. It's an absolutely elegant treatment for preserving small family trinkets and tiny treasures. Use glue to hold the items in place. The panel and the edges are trimmed with upholstery braid. ∾

Flower Pillow

A pressed pink bluebell blossom was photocopied and transferred using the iron-on method to a piece of silk organza. The organza was backed with blue fabric to make a panel, and the panel was inserted in a pillow top of brushed felt. Decorative machine stitching surrounds the panel. Upholstery braid edges the pillow. ∾

Pictured from left: Flower Pillow, Dusty Rose Treasure Pillow

PHOTO PILLOWS

This pillow shows a collage of photos accented with decorative buttons and transfers of pressed flowers.
Iron-on transfer paper was used. See the Techniques section for step-by-step instructions.

Sometimes one photo is all you need. Transfer medium was used to transfer the photos to pieces of white fabric. the pieces of fabric where then sewn in place on the pillow forms. See the Techniques section for step-by-step instructions.

WALL HANGING

Simple quilting skills can be employed to fashion a commemorative wall hanging for anniversaries and championship celebrations.

Here, photographs, news clippings, a cartoon, and crests were photocopied on iron-on transfer paper and transferred to cream and beige cotton fabric. The transfers were sewn on the brushed felt backing, and coordinating gingham and solids were pieced to make frames and backgrounds for the transfers. The same fabrics were pieced to form a border for the hanging with mitered corners. Felt loops at the top of the hanging were added to slip over a wooden rod for display.

Pins, buttons, and ribbons can be attached to the hanging for extra interest and color. ∞

Jewelry & Wearable Memories

Memory jewelry can tell a story with family photos, precious trinkets, and mementos. Jewelry pieces make very special gifts that sparkle with the past. Being able to transfer photographs to aprons, T-shirts, and tote bags opens up gift possibilities for everyone on your list!

MEMENTO NECKLACES

Charm and bead companies have made it easy for us to create fashionable memory jewelry with frame charms, theme charms, and a huge selection of beautiful beads and jewelry findings. Wear them individually or collected on a chain. Tiny photos in frames are lovely, as are pieces of broken china wrapped with silver tape and wire.

VINTAGE CHARMS SILVER NECKLACE

When designing your necklace, place the larger and heavier pieces at the center of the chain and the smaller pieces near the ends.

You'll Need

- Sterling silver chain, your choice of length
- Selection of silver charms to fit your theme
- Mother-of-pearl heart beads
- Sterling silver wire (available at lapidary stores and bead stores)
- Mementos (reduced photocopies of favorite photographs, pieces of broken china, mother-of-pearl buttons, vintage beads, and bits of vintage lace)
- Jewelry findings, including silver jump rings and head pins
- Round nosed pliers
- Strong jewelry glue
- Metallic silver adhesive backed paper (found at rubber stamp stores or fine art stores)

Here's How

1. Place photocopies of photos or old letters or actual bits of lace in the frame charm.
2. Wrap sharp edges of bits of broken china with tiny strips of metallic silver adhesive backed paper or carefully sand the sharp edges of the china with emery paper. Wrap a small piece of silver wire around the china piece, making small loops at the top and bottom with round nose pliers. On the bottom loop, hang a charm with a jump ring.
3. To hang the buttons, loop a small piece of silver wire through the holes and curl the ends to hold the button. Fashion a loop just above the top of the button to hang on the chain with a jump ring.
4. Thread beads on silver head pins and form a loop at the top. Fasten the loops to the chain. ᴄᴏ

Pictured from left: Mementos can be worn individually on cords or chains or attached to a more substantial chain to make the Vintage Charms Silver Necklace.

BUTTONS

Machine washable buttons can be fashioned to accent your clothes with photos. Use large shank buttons and glue photos to the top using white glue. When dry, sand off the excess paper and coat the covered buttons with white glue to seal, then cover with a pour-on resin coating.

Tips
- Have the buttons ready for coating when you are using the resin coating on larger objects – you can use the small amounts of resin that are left over from other projects to cover the buttons.
- Let the resin set up at least 12 hours. Then add a second coat for extra insurance that the buttons will last through many washings.
- To make button covers, cut off the shanks of the buttons with a pair of wire cutters and glue the buttons to button covers. (Photo button covers look great on cuff buttons.)

Decorative Theme Pin

Look at your favorite craft or bead store for pins with loops for hanging theme charms. You can choose charms that tell the story of the person in the photograph for a truly personalized gift. This pin with a photo of my mom in a silver charm frame is adorned with sewing charms to celebrate her sewing and quilting talents. A spool charm was wrapped with silver wire and glued at the top of the pin. ∾

95

MICA LAPEL PINS

These lightweight pins make a beautiful statement as they grace your lapel. I used black and white photographs to make the photocopies for the ones shown on the right, but hand-tinted copies and color photos also make wonderful sparkling pins.

You'll Need

- Mica sheets, pieces up to 3" long
- Reduced photocopies of favorite photographs
- Gold and silver bouillon (found at craft, florist, and Christmas stores – bouillon was used at the turn of the century to wrap Christmas ornaments and as tinsel on trees. It comes tightly coiled and you stretch it to make the sparkling, kinky wire. Substitute fine beading wire if you cannot locate bouillon.)
- White craft glue
- Silicone jewelry glue
- Pin back
- Accents (glass beads and fine beading wire, charms, small dried flowers)
- Sharp scissors

Here's How

1. Cut mica sheets to the size and shape desired. Use decorative edge scissors if you wish.
2. Split the mica sheet into two identical layers. Arrange the photocopy (and dried flowers, if you wish) on one mica sheet. When you are pleased with the arrangement, use a little white glue to adhere the design elements in place.
3. Place the other mica sheet on top and glue, laminating the copies and flowers in between.
4. With a pair of sharp scissors, cut six to seven tiny notches around the edge of the pin.
5. Wrap the pin with bouillon, passing the bouillon through the notches, twisting the ends together to hold.
6. If you wish to use beads, thread them on fine beading wire and wrap around the pin. Glue charms with silicone glue.
7. Glue the pin back in place with silicone glue. ∽

KEY CHAIN

Here's one way Grandma won't lose her keys! Decoupage a photocopy on a 2-1/2" diameter wooden disc. Sand the edges to clean off the excess paper. Paint the edges with silver paint and let dry. Seal the copy with a coat of white glue. Let dry. Cover the key chain with the pour-on resin for durability. When the resin has set up and is completely dry, drill a small hole and add a silver split ring.

Reunion Photo Shirt

*A group photo transferred to a T-shirt becomes
the focal point for this whimsical shirt that celebrates
the family.*

Here's How

Step One: Copying and Transferring

This family photo was copied on transfer paper, cut out
carefully around the people, and ironed on the shirt. When
working directly on a ready made garment, always test to
make sure the fabric and color are suitable for your transfer.
I do the test on the inside back of the shirt.

Step Two: Adding Painted Embellishments

The family name, reunion date, or an inspirational saying
can be added with dimensional fabric paint. The paints are
easy to use, and children can use them to decorate their own
shirts. A few whimsical wiggles and zig-zags are all that's
needed. ∽

KITCHEN APRON

Photos of food preparation and people eating look great on a chef's canvas apron.

You'll Need

- A canvas apron
- An assortment of photos copied on iron-on transfer paper
- Food theme stencils (I used cookies, fruit, and cinnamon sticks.)
- Alphabet stencil
- Stencil gels
- Foam stencil applicator or stencil brush

Here's How

1. Arrange the photos and iron to transfer.
2. Stencil food motifs with stencil gels.
3. Stencil a saying at the top with the alphabet stencil. ∞

TOTE BAG

This canvas tote bag makes a wonderful gift for a knitter or quilter.

You'll Need

- A canvas tote bag
- An assortment of children's photos copied on iron-on transfer paper
- Patterned stencils (prints that simulate printed fabric)
- Stencil gels
- Foam stencil applicator or stencil brush
- Black fine tip permanent marker

Here's How

1. Arrange the photos and iron to transfer.
2. Stencil printed "patches" with stencil gels.
3. Add stitching details and journaling with a black permanent marker. ∽

Gifts & Wraps

PICTURE PUZZLES

Many copy centers can turn your photograph into a puzzle. It makes a great gift, especially for the child in the photo. Place the puzzle pieces in a box with a copy of the complete photo glued to the box top.

You also can make puzzle greeting cards by using a glue stick to adhere a photocopy to the top of a blank puzzle card. When the glue has dried, carefully cut the photocopy with an art knife.

A puzzle card.

102

Pictured at right: Photo puzzles in boxes.

GREETING CARDS

*Greeting cards, gift tags, postcards, and placecards
are fun for the whole family to make. I love to place
photo cards in vellum envelopes to softly mute the colors
of the card inside.
Use these examples as guides for creating your
own cards with your family's photographs.*

You'll Need

• Lots of photocopies, on both bond paper and vellum
• Colorful card stock paper
• Decorative edge scissors
• A glue stick

Also useful:
• A slide trimmer
• Bone folder, for making neat folds in card stock
• Stick-on or glue-on photo corners
• Image transfer pens
• Paint pens

Welcome Baby!
A smile from a
is packaged

It's your Birthday!

Photo Stamps and Placecards

Entertaining photo stamps are a wonderful accent for envelopes and, pasted on card stock, they make sweet little gift cards. Photocopy and reduce photos, if needed. Cut out and adhere to white paper with a glue stick. Use stamp edge decorative scissors to create the perforated-look edges. For gift cards or placecards, glue on card stock.
To make "lick and stick" stamps, *mix 1 part white vinegar with 2 parts white glue. Paint on the back of the stamps with a brush. Let dry. To use, moisten the glue and stick the stamp down.* ❧

Wire Holders

Wonderful wire holders for image transfer placecards can be easily twisted from craft wire.

You'll Need

- 1 yd. black wire, 28 gauge
- 1 yd. copper wire, 28 gauge
- A pencil

Here's How

1. Fold the wire in half to form a four strand-length 18" long.
2. Fold the wire in half around a pencil and start to twist. When you have twisted all the wire, you will have approximately an 8" length.
3. Measure 3-1/2" from the loops and bend into a spiral to form the base of the stand.
4. Remove the loops from the pencil. Pull apart to form the holder for the card. ❧

PHOTO GIFT BAGS

*Don't forget to make the gift packaging as memorable
as the gift. These gift bags were adorned with
photocopies and accented with ribbon, paint pens,
and polymer clay seals.*

Kraft Paper Vintage Gift Bag

A gold paint pen was used to write "Memories" over and over in diagonal lines. A sepia-toned oval photocopy was cut out with decorative edge scissors and glued on the bag. ∾

Sisters Gift Bag

A black and white photo was copied on glossy paper, cut out with decorative edge scissors, and glued to a glossy white gift bag. A black permanent marker was used to write "Sisters are forever friends" around the photo. ∾

Three Children Gift Bag

Decorative edge scissors were used to cut the top edge of a plain white paper bag. A length of crimson ribbon – with the ends left long for tying – was glued around the bag. A vintage photo was reduced, copied, and cut out with the same decorative edge scissors used to cut the top. The photo was glued on top of the ribbon, and a black polymer clay seal was stamped, embellished with gold paint, and glued on the ribbon. ∾

GIFT BOXES

The swirl top box was made using purchased box templates found at a rubber stamp store. A pattern is included for the pillow box. It can be reduced to create a smaller box. They're just the right size to hold a small picture or a piece of jewelry. I used monotone photocopies, positioned them on the flat box templates, and adhered them to the box templates with a glue stick. When the glue was dry I trimmed the edges with a craft knife. A length of iridescent ribbon adds a finishing touch to the pillow boxes and holds the ends securely. ✎

See pillow box pattern on page 125.

Ornaments

Ornaments are a wonderful way to remember special times and special people. In the pages that follow, you'll see a variety of ideas for using photographs to create charming keepsake ornaments.

PENNY PHOTO ORNAMENTS

I call these penny ornaments because the templates for making all the sizes and shapes are circles. A number of creative variations are possible with this easy technique.

CIRCLE PENNY ORNAMENTS

You'll Need

- Photocopies of favorite photographs
- Circle cutter or circle template
- Glue stick
- Colored card stock paper
- Brass wire or thin wire-edge ribbon for hanger
- *Optional:* Bouillon, glass head pins, metallic paint pens

Here's How

1. Cut out all the circles for your ornament. A circle cutter makes this task easy and fast.
2. Trace a triangle within each circle. If you are planning to make several ornaments, it saves time to cut a template of heavy card stock and trace around it. Plan the photo placement carefully. (You don't want the people to be upside down!) Measure twice and cut once.
3. Fold along the traced lines in each circle. Decide whether you are going to construct a winged penny ornament or a diamond penny ornament. (See next page.)
4. Glue the triangles together with a glue stick. Use clips to hold while drying, if necessary.
5. To accent your ornament, dip glass

Circle Penny Ornaments in three sizes.

pins into white craft glue then into the points on your ornament. To add an extra sparkle, wrap bouillon around the pins or around the ornament wings.
6. Fashion a hanger by making a small loop out of brass wire. Dip the ends in white glue and push into the top of the ornament.
7. Thread the loop with a piece of ribbon to make the ornament ready to hang. (Large winged penny ornaments can sit on a surface, so they don't have to have hangers.) ∾

DIAMOND PENNY ORNAMENTS

Diamond Penny Ornaments are a variation of the Circle Penny Ornament. They are made the same way, but the flaps of the circles are glued to the inside, creating the diamond shape.

Variations for Penny Ornaments

• The sizes of the circles you start with determine the size of your finished ornament. For example, 3" circles make an ornament 5" high, 2-1/2" circles make an ornament 3-1/2" high, and 2" circles make an ornament 3" high.

• You can vary the number of circles in an ornament for different looks and shapes. The photo of the Circle Penny Ornaments shows ornaments made with six circles, eight circles, and ten circles.

• You need not use photographs for each circle. You can alternate with card stock circles on which you can write inspirational sayings, names, or dates.

MEMORY BALLS

*These special keepsake ornaments are easily made with clear plastic shapes
that snap together to encase mementos.*

You'll Need

- Clear plastic ornaments (found at craft stores in all sizes and shapes)
- Filler material (tulle, Spanish moss, a felt ball filled with a little polyester fiberfill, etc.)
- Small treasures (frame charms with photocopy of a favorite photograph, charms, buttons, old lace, ribbon roses, alphabet beads, beaded initial, dried flowers from a special day)
- Thin ribbon to glue on the seam
- Ribbon for hanger and bow
- White craft glue or glue gun and glue sticks

Here's How

1. Snap the ornament apart. Fill one half with your chosen filler. Use a little glue to hold it in place.
2. Arrange your trinkets on the top of the filler, using glue to hold them in place.
3. Carefully place the other half on top and snap to hold.
4. Glue a thin ribbon along the seam to hold the ornament firmly together.
5. Make a multi-loop bow and glue in place on the top.
6. Thread a loop of ribbon through the top hole and tie to create the hanger. Additional charms, rosebuds, or buttons can be glued into the bow for accents. ∞

Jocelyn Ornament, Baby B Ornament

Pictured right: Rose Ornament, Autumn Ornament

CERAMIC BABY ORNAMENTS

Photocopies are glued to the inside well of these ready made glazed ceramic pieces to make these cute photo ornaments.

You'll Need

- Ceramic ornament
- Color photocopy of photo
- Embellishments (buttons, charms, rosebuds)
- White glue
- Strong jewelry glue
- Two-part pour-on resin coating
- Ribbon

Here's How

1. Cut the copy to fit the well in the ornament. Glue in place, Let dry.
2. Seal the copy with white glue.
3. Glue on buttons, charms, and trinkets in place with strong jewelry glue.
4. Mix resin according to manufacturer's instructions and pour in the well to create the high gloss finish. Let set.
5. Finish the ornament by adding a multi-looped bow and ribbon hanger. Decorate the bow with additional charms. ∞

BALSA FRAME ORNAMENTS

Hang these ornaments in a window and create your own slide show. The designs are simple and easy to make.

You'll Need

- Balsa wood strips, 1/4" square, to frame the prints (the largest ornament uses only a 12" length of wood)
- Mini saw and miter box
- Photocopied prints of your favorite photographs (If you wish to make the ornament transparent, photocopy the photos on vellum.)
- Two-part pour-on resin coating
- Mini brass screw eyes
- White craft glue
- Short pins
- Ribbon for hangers
- Metallic craft paint
- Paint brush
- Sandpaper

Here's How

1. Determine the size of frame you will need by cropping the photo to size.
2. Cut the balsa wood strips with the mini saw and miter box.
3. Glue the strips together with white glue to form the frame. Reinforce each corner with a pin.
4. Paint the frames with metallic paint. Let dry.
5. Glue the photocopy to the back of the frame. Let dry. Sand the edges to make the paper flush with the wooden edges.
6. Seal the photocopies with a coat of white glue. (You can omit this step if your photocopies are on vellum.)
7. Mix the resin coating. Pour the resin into the frames and let set.
8. Attach a brass screw eye at the top of the frame.
9. Tie on the ribbon hanger and bow. ⟳

POLYMER CLAY ORNAMENTS

Bows and charms accent these images on polymer clay. They're quick and easy to make. For complete instructions, see "Transferring Images to Polymer Clay." Add bows in coordinating colors and charms to complete and secure with glue when the ornaments have cooled. ∾

PHOTOS UNDER GLASS ORNAMENTS

*Follow the general directions for placing
photos under glass in the techniques section.
Small beveled glass pieces make a charming
ornament finished with an elegant bow.
Dried flowers, bits of old lace, pieces of letters,
and other mementos can be included.* ∾

PATTERN FOR PILLOW BOX
SEE PAGE 110 FOR INSTRUCTIONS AND PHOTO

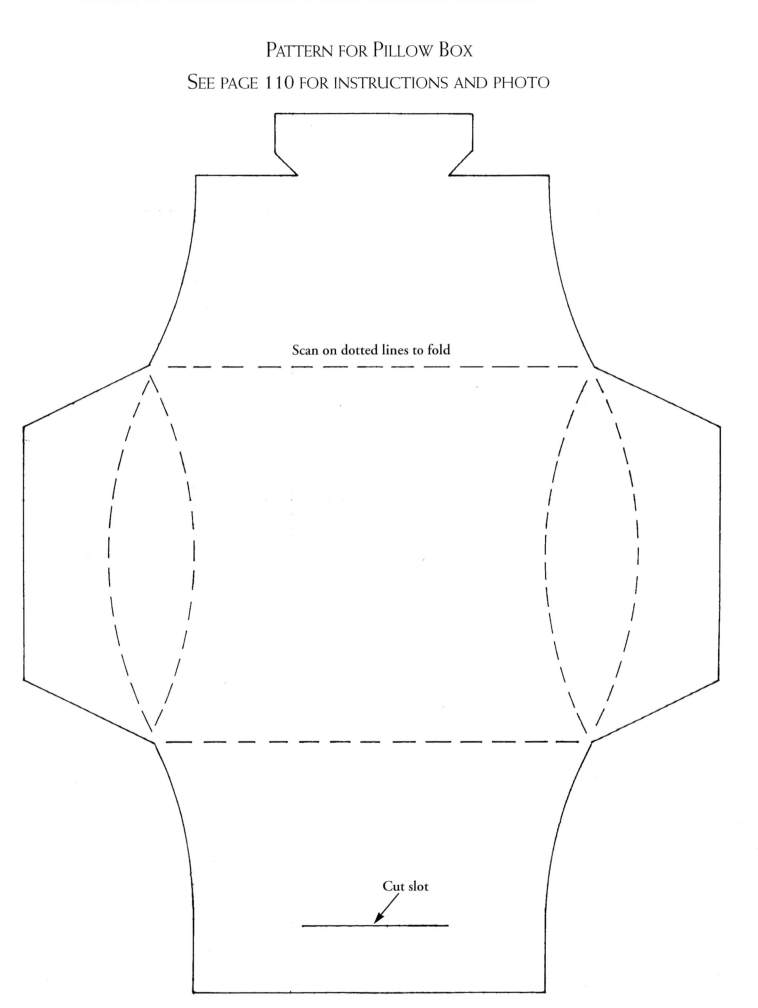

Scan on dotted lines to fold

Cut slot

METRIC CONVERSION CHART

INCHES TO MILLIMETERS AND CENTIMETERS

Inches	MM	CM
1/8	3	.3
1/4	6	.6
3/8	10	1.0
1/2	13	1.3
5/8	16	1.6
3/4	19	1.9
7/8	22	2.2
1	25	2.5
1-1/4	32	3.2
1-1/2	38	3.8
1-3/4	44	4.4
2	51	5.1
3	76	7.6
4	102	10.2
5	127	12.7
6	152	15.2
7	178	17.8
8	203	20.3
9	229	22.9
10	254	25.4
11	279	27.9
12	305	30.5

YARDS TO METERS

Yards	Meters
1/8	.11
1/4	.23
3/8	.34
1/2	.46
5/8	.57
3/4	.69
7/8	.80
1	.91
2	1.83
3	2.74
4	3.66
5	4.57
6	5.49
7	6.40
8	7.32
9	8.23
10	9.14

INDEX

A
Albums (see photo albums) 38

B
Baby Door Sign 54
Balsa Frame Ornaments 120
Boxes & Albums for Photos & Memories 34
Buttons 94

C
Calendars 82, 84
Candles 20, 78, 81
Ceramic Baby Ornaments 118
Clay pots 50
Coaster Tray 60
Coasters 57
Collage Tray 58
Collecting 10
Color tinting 16
Crackling 29
Cropping 12
Cutting 12
Cutting tools 12

D
Decorative paint 28
Decorative Photo Plates 40
Decorative Theme Pin 95
Decoupage 21, 68
Desk Pad and Pen Holder 48
Desk screen 46
Diamond Penny Ornaments 114
Documenting 11

F
Fabric Memories 86, 88, 90
Flocking 29
Flower Faces on Clay Pots 50
Frames 64, 66, 76
Framing & Displaying Photos 64

G
Gift Boxes 110
Gifts & Wraps 102, 104, 106, 108, 110
Glass 26, 72, 124
Greeting Cards 104

I
Image Transfer Calendar 84

J
Jewelry & Wearable Memories 92, 94, 95, 96, 98, 100, 101
Journaling 11

K
Kitchen Apron 100

L
Labeling 11
Light Switch Plates 56

M
Magnets 80
Memento Necklaces 92
Memory Balls 116
Memory Candles 81
Memory Shadow Boxes 70
Mica 27, 96
Mica Lapel Pins 96

INDEX

N
Night light 55

O
Organizing, 10
Ornaments 112, 114, 116, 118, 120, 122, 124

P
Pattern for Pillow Box 125
Penny Photo Ornaments 112
Photo albums 38
Photo Gift Bags
Photo plates 40
Photo Pillows 88
Photo Stamps and Placecards 106
Photo storage boxes 34, 36,
Photocopying 14, 15
Photos on Canvas 74
Photos Under Glass 72, 124
Photos Under Glass Ornaments 124
Picture Puzzles 102
Pillows 86, 88
Polymer clay 18, 76, 122
Polymer Clay Frames 76
Polymer Clay Ornaments 122
Preserving 10, 11
Preserving flowers 30
Puzzles 102

R
Reunion Photo Shirt 98
Resin 22, 23
Rubber stamping 28

S
Scanning 15
School Days Calendar 82
Seaside Memory & Vacation Wreath 42
Seaside Memory Frame 64
Shadow Boxes 70
Sleeping Elves Night Light 55
Stack of Coasters 57
Stackable Blocks 52
Stenciling 28

T
Three-D Decoupage Photos 68
Three Panel Desk Screen 46
Tile Trivet 62
Tools, cutting 12
Tote Bag 101
Transferring 17, 18, 24, 84
Trays and Coasters 57, 58, 60

U
Using Memories in Home Decor 40

V
Vintage Charms Silver Necklace 92
Vintage Open Book Arrangement 44
Votive Candle Lamps 78

W
Wall Hanging 90
Wooden Frame for Dad 66
Wreath 42